3D Printing Design

3D Printing Design

Additive Manufacturing and the Materials Revolution

Francis Bitonti

BLOOMSBURY VISUAL ARTS
LONDON • NEW YORK • OXFORD • NEW DELHI • SYDNEY

BLOOMSBURY VISUAL ARTS
Bloomsbury Publishing Plc
50 Bedford Square, London, WC1B 3DP, UK
1385 Broadway, New York, NY 10018, USA

BLOOMSBURY, BLOOMSBURY VISUAL ARTS and the Diana logo are
trademarks of Bloomsbury Publishing Plc

First published in Great Britain 2019

Cover design: Adriana Brioso
Cover image © United Nude

A catalogue record for this book is available from the British Library.

A catalog record for this book is available from the Library of Congress.

ISBN:	HB:	978-1-3500-6552-9
	PB:	978-1-4742-2096-5
	ePDF:	978-1-4742-2097-2
	eBook:	978-1-3500-3219-4

Typeset by RefineCatch Limited, Bungay, Suffolk
Printed and bound in India

To find out more about our authors and books visit www.bloomsbury.com
and sign up for our newsletters.

This book is dedicated to my parents, Maria Bitonti and Frank Bitonti. Thank you for teaching me to have the perseverance and confidence necessary to bring the impossible into the world, each and every day, and for teaching me that any other life would be unacceptable.

I would like to make a special note to my father, Frank Michael Bitonti, who left this world on August 7, 2012. Thank you for living a life that has always been and always will be my greatest teacher. You lived a life of unapologetic bravery, sincerity, and generosity. You touched more lives than you will ever know.

CONTENTS

ACKNOWLEDGMENTS

I have been extremely lucky in my career to be surrounded by an amazing team of people whose contributions to generative design and additive manufacturing have been substantial and have greatly influenced my intellectual and professional life. To the team in my office without whom this book and our many accomplishments would not be possible Peter Wildfeuer and Li Chen, and a special thank you to Madison Maxey for her contributions to this process.

I would also like to thank everyone who lent me their time and knowledge while putting together this book.

Introduction

Material is media.

I have listened to many designers over the last few years talk about "the next industrial revolution." This language is misdirecting and counterproductive. We need to be designing for the information revolution. Designers are now able to think through computational processes and solve evermore complex problems in increasingly efficient and elegant ways. It is the thesis of this book that the Information Age has brought designers and engineers to the threshold of a materials revolution by giving us more capacity to design with complexity and variation. This book is intended to give designers an access point to understand this new industrial landscape whilst it is developing, and at the same time to learn the hard skills and mathematical concepts to integrate generative algorithms and additive fabrication tools into your design methodology. I started writing this book under the assumption that it will be impossible for the next generation of manufacturing and material technologies to take shape unless designers learn to think through computation as their medium. The chapters that follow have been written to help you understand the emerging trends and possible futures that will be the result of these new technologies and better position design methodologies within this changing landscape.

If you are new to additive manufacturing, the first three chapters provide a foundation in the main issues: the practical reach of hardware; the user-friendliness (or not) of software; and the various business models that are beginning to take shape. Finally, Chapter 4 presents case studies from Studio Bitonti, three from the world of fashion, one from the medical industry, and a brief furniture case study.

The reader should note that I began writing this book in 2012. This work and the opinions of the author reflect the very earliest ideas that motivated the founding of Studio Bitonti in New York. Much has changed since I started writing this book. I was a passionate and young designer who was extremely idealistic. However, the opinions and the work highlighted in this book still influence our thinking at the office today and how we approach design and engineering challenges. This book is important because it captures the mindset around what I hope was a very important early body of work.

I hope this book will read as a manifesto and conceptual guide for how we think about digital design and digital fabrication.

1

The materials revolution of 3D printing

Also called "additive manufacturing," 3D printing refers to any fabrication technology that builds up a construction by an additive process rather than by subtraction. Subtraction, in this sense, refers to the cutting and carving of standard blocks of material, subtracting from the block. Crafting and designing something has heretofore been a matter of subtraction. Additive manufacturing, on the other hand, builds up materials layer by layer, even particle by particle. It is a process of building up rather than subtracting.

Materials and tools have long been subject to a linear progression building on top of the other. We have experienced through the ages a successive linear evolution of our capacities since the first wood tools were made. With primitive tools, we made other wood tools and with those tools we made stone tools. And this progression goes on and on through the ages, from the Stone Age to the Steel Age to the Information Age. The tools of the Information Age will no longer be formed by handheld tools and human intuition, which since the dawn of civilization has been the case. Our tools expand our capacity to form and manipulate present materials. These tools define our creative capacities as human beings. Tools define our culture at any particular point in history, as well as the materials those tools enable us to manipulate. For example, the work of architect Ludwig Mies van der Rohe could never have existed in the Bronze Age, it would have been impossible to form such lightweight structures. We had to wait until we mastered steel, aluminum, and glass for such structures to exist in the world. Even if Rohe were to have lived at that time, the available tools and resources could never have enabled such a vision for our current built environment. For the first time ever, our tools for manipulating matter are linguistic and driven by the cultivation and replication of information. Language is now our hammer and saw, data our medium. This means product design, architecture, and fashion design are now all linguistic activities, capable of benefiting from the distributed models we have seen in the Information Age. Materials are now flexible, malleable things that start as data capable of being formed, shared, and edited in a digital environment. We can presently remix objects; materials are like a video or a song. Everything discussed in this book stems from a radical way of thinking about how we design with materials.

Additive manufacturing also presents us with an entirely unique material condition to design for: we are now in a position to build up objects, micron by micron, with an ever increasing amount of control over the geometry on both the micro- and macro-scales. This new capacity is, for now, largely hindered by (at the time of writing this book) not yet having adequate design software that enables us to manipulate technologies in this way, although that day is rapidly approaching. This chapter will argue that the greatest advancements in materials for 3D printing will largely be software driven. First, let us examine in more detail this material revolution.

3D printers and computational modeling processes have unlocked a completely new understanding of materials for us. Computational modeling and imaging technologies have expanded our capacity to represent the world around us by producing evermore robust drawings and visualizations. We are now able to draw the most complex geometries, both real and imagined. Initially, there was a gap between these software-driven advancements and the tools for manifesting these visions into tangible material. 3D printers close the gap between representation and fabrication. To draw is to make, and the separation between the two continues to close.

UNDERSTANDING FORMULAS IN COMPUTATION

Computational Design often utilizes rules and relationships inherent in mathematical equations to generate iterations. A mathematical expression in this book consists of three different parts: variables, constants, and an output. "Variables" are numbers that can vary based on circumstance. "Constants" are numbers that remain constant in the equation no matter the circumstance, and the output is the result of the calculation.

It could be argued that materials are now digital constructs. Materials are no longer analog things, but digital assets whose construction and organization are largely subject to the capacities of our current software. We are living through a technological revolution that is bringing about significant cultural, social, and economic transformation. 3D printing, more specifically "additive manufacturing," is reinventing our capacities for engaging with physical matter. Products are now digital assets. To "make" is now to produce temporal, transformable, editable, and self-replicating entities, capable of having an equally rich life in the digital environment as they have enjoyed in the physical environment. Matter is now media.

KEY TERMS

Slicer, Tool Path, and G-Code are the three terms that describe the moment of translation to form geometric representation instructions for a tool. Passing through the slicer and exporting a geometry as G-Code represents a moment of translation from physical to digital.

Slicer

A Slicer is computer program that converts a three-dimensional CAD (Computer-Aided Design) model into instructions that the 3D printer will follow so that it deposits material in the correct way and achieves the desired form and material effects.

Tool Path

A Tool Path is a term used to describe a set of vectors that indicate the motion of a tool through space.

G-Code

The G-Code is the programming language used to tell the 3D printer what to do. The slicer converts your CAD file into strings of commands written in G-Code that describes tool paths. G-Code contains more than vectors, also including information like temptation of the tool, speed of travel, and a variety of other commands that control the motors and tools in a particular machine.

A complex kind of media

If our material world is influenced by formation of the digital or software environment, then we can start to think about physical material as a kind of digital media. And, if matter is media, that means it is compressible, shareable, hackable, downloadable, can be open-sourced, light, and highly disposable and capable of self-replication. In a world such as this, we need to reinvent the way we think about material construction from a digital perspective. We need to rethink how we understand the design of new materials. How we design new material constructions, but, more importantly, what are the kinds of systems of representation we need in order to access and manipulate that data which will lead us to new forms and new material compositions?

A good starting point of reference is medical imaging. Medical imaging has had to address this problem, except those creating medical imaging software had to do the reverse. They had to take lots of really complex organic material organizations and find ways of indexing and representing all these different materials. Imaging biological systems within the medical community meant having to take various and differentiated physical components and digitally rendering them into high resolution. We are enabled to create these images in the inverse method through 3D printing and additive manufacturing.

EARLY WORKS

When I first began working, I was an architect. Due to the nature of the materials and the technologies that I was working with, I gradually became interested in product design and eventually in fashion. My first project when I set out on my own was a proposal for a bike rack for the New York City Department of Transportation (Figure 1.1). I was selected as a finalist for a competition and was commissioned to produce two prototypes of my idea. I submitted a set of drawings that was, in all honesty, designed more as a provocation than as something I expected to have built and installed in the city. The geometries could not be fabricated by traditional means and was rapidly going way out of budget on research and development (R&D) trying to find a way to produce a set of geometries that were not traditionally machineable—until I discovered 3D printing. It was clear to me that there could be no other medium to suit my design methodology. My design methodology had evolved before manufacturing had discovered ways to interface with the means of representation that I was working with in my design process. I was able to draw more and calculate more than I was enabled to communicate to the machines and fabrication professionals I was working with. It was clear that I had to learn to bridge the gap.

Early in my career, I learned a lot about what software could do for designers. I saw that software could enable me to draw and manage data for thousands, if not millions, of individual, very complex, designs—all uniquely generated by an algorithm. I learned that I could produce geometries that did not adhere to any of the principles of form-making that I had learned in school. On paper, it seemed like the digital revolution had come, and it had for designers. The models of representation I had learned as a design student had been blown away. However, the revolution had not yet come for the manufacturing equipment and the people who would be making my work. My studio finished the bike rack going about $40,000 out

FIGURE 1.1 Bike Rack Prototype for the NY City Racks: The New York City Department of Transportation (DOT), in partnership with the Cooper-Hewitt National Design Museum and the support of Google Inc. and Transportation Alternatives.

of budget. Obviously, this did not become the new bike rack for New York City, only one was temporarily installed at Astor Place.

I realized at this time that I had to focus on actualizing these geometries through industrial manufacturing. The designs I was producing were a catalyst in anticipation of a material world that had not been created yet. The next five years of my life were to be spent trying to pioneer techniques to make this future of mass customization and complex differentiating material composites a reality. I knew it could be described digitally, and I knew that machines could be controlled digitally. The next few years for me would be about trying to remove tooling. This chapter is about the material revolution designers of my generation have strived to instigate.

Designers today are being presented with an opportunity to take on a grand project that will reach far beyond aesthetics and form and function. It is an opportunity to redefine not only the relationship of function and form, but also the interfaces with design and fabrication tools and the structure of manufacturing infrastructure. It is an opportunity not simply to make more stuff, but to redefine what "stuff" is. As I will describe in the next chapter, industrial manufacturing has left us with a very specific understanding of material that has led to influencing the way we approach markets. An approach that is bound to evolve as design and manufacturing move to the cloud—the end of modernism and all that goes with that paradigm. Modularity and standardization will be replaced with mass customization in the years ahead. Design movements since modernism have been very subtle movements brought about through the history of various design disciplines, like postmodernism, largely dominated by internal discussions about the language of design. Since the crystallization of modernism and the industrial age, designers have been playing games with formal languages but have not had the opportunity to invent entirely new languages until now.

It is now possible to question the most fundamental principles of the discipline. Manufacturing is being rebuilt, and the flows of material and commerce redirected. It is a blank canvas, free from the shackles of history and expectations, a blissful space without memories and only a bright future. This could be the generation that will redefine materiality. Brands will no longer dictate trends, but be forced to become platforms for co-creation, as will be discussed further on in this chapter. This is the last step in the evolution towards a decimalized world, and designers are to be the ones to take us across the finish line. All of these transformations are strongly tied to the changes in the ways we both draw and produce material qualities and performance.

Our visualization, design, and manufacturing tools are expanding human capacities to design new continuously differentiated material composites on from our computers. This is the foundation of all changes being put forward by 3D printing, a technology that greatly expands our capacity to work with materials. It expands our capacities through computational processes, therefore subjecting advancement of our ability to manipulate material to the pressures of Moore's law (that technology and computation has exponential growth over time). We are moving from a world in which materials, tools, and objects are produced and evolved by an analog means into a world where materials, tools, and objects are processed and evolved by digital means. For example, the tools we use at Studio Bitonti let us compute and simulate hundreds of thousands of forms in the cloud at once. We understand the full possibility space of any design problem. Computation keeps us from having to hunt in the dark for the best solution.

As a result of these technologies, materials themselves are relational and linguistic.

When I say materials are built on sets of relationships that are linguistic, I am referring to the use of programing languages to set up structural relationships that generate data that can then be used to form objects. The act of fabrication becomes a byproduct of systems that more or less operate as coded language. The computer code sets up a logical framework that generates geometry and the geometry is used to program the means of production. The geometry is a go-between for different languages. The digitization of the manufacturing process results in a definition of matter that can be evolved through language. The 3D printer is a platform for the formation of matter that can be controlled and manipulated by language and that is capable of being networked. 3D printers are capable of producing so much variety because they operate by logic, rooted in the additive of a series of discrete entities. The next generation of machines will accept vectors and points and can learn new programs quickly, without slow and expensive efforts to program new designs. This allows form to emerge from a series of localized interactions. The tool itself has few formal tendencies. The architect Luis Kahn once asked, "What does the brick want to be?" Today, we can only ask what the pixel, voxel, or vector wants to be. We have replaced components with fundamental elements for describing geometry. Tools and therefore matter have no formal tendencies. A 3D printer is a generic non-specific tool that is also capable of self-replication. 3D printers have discretized matter and, as a result, assembly of physical form and material differentiation no longer falls on the tool but on the manipulation of a codified language. This is a paradigm shift. This means materials are now shaped by linguistic constructs (computer programing languages) rather than formations of other materials. Material formation is increasingly being informed by sets of digital instructions that are forming machine processes, used to form matter.

3D printing is highly versatile but, most importantly, it gives us a stronger connection to software interfaces. It operates by language; it's a codified and standardized way of describing materials and machine operations. Materials will one day be thought of as buttons we press in CAD applications. It transforms materials into linguistic constructs with a clearly defined protocol for editing, sharing, and production. It is a generic technology with a limited set of parameters capable of being controlled by a language—this is what enables the great diversity of output. Standardization at these lower levels of how we describe materials and production processes is what allows something to be both consistently reproduced across many different machines and also to be easily understood and edited by others. It allows for the production of physical things to be described purely with patterns and not rely on geometry or specific material organizations. 3D printing, and its reliance on code for production, makes a differently structured set of relationships between the designer, the manufacture, and the tool.

Microscopic control

One of the biggest paradigm shifts that is taking place as a result of this technology is that we now have the capacity to manipulate materials and structures at what is ever quickly approaching a near microscopic level. In order to manage that complexity, it will be necessary to augment perception through digital visualization tools. These tools are going to play a key role in enabling us to analyze and design clearly, despite the complexity. The ability to manipulate large amounts of highly differentiated data is one of the most significant creative capacities computation affords us as human beings. As a result, this greatly redefines our capacity to form matter through digitally controlled fabrication technologies like 3D printers. In many ways, the 3D printer is a byproduct of computational technologies. As we will see from the case studies in the following chapters, there are a significant number of parallels between digital methods for graphic representation and various printing technologies. Successfully manipulating the means of representation often leads to material innovation as the two are inextricably linked. This ability to manipulate large datasets in combination with a production medium that is digitally controlled is one of the key ingredients in defining our capacity to form matter in the Information Age. In the examples provided later on, we are looking to define what those new capacities are. In understanding what new capacities these technologies enable, we can best understand what new trends will emerge as a result of these new capacities.

Precomputation designers had to work with materials that were themselves packaged and sold as standardized products. I do not mean to suggest that the information-driven manufacturing will put an end to productized or even standardized materials. However, materials will be standardized at the micro- and not the macro-level. Currently, fabric comes in long, standardized sheets, and woods and metals are sold in blocks and bars that come in standardized sizes. We design and fabricate components through subtractive processes. It is rare that the designer of a product has the opportunity to design the materials used to create the product. 3D printing allows the designer to work with materials in a much more fluid and deeper way. Predefined sizes or properties are no longer a consideration as we have replaced subtraction with addition and are able to print objects that do not have a consistent cross section. A result of this is that gradients of material properties are now a possibility, and the only standard dimensions we need to be mindful of is the size of the build volume of the printer, and even this can be overcome through the intelligent design of printers.

I always tend to laugh when I see people who are selling materials in bulk that are 3D printed. Why would you do that? I laugh because what they are doing is forcing 3D printing technology into a standardized means of production. They are forcing material culture back into the industrial paradigm, which is to create materials that have consistent properties throughout, when, really, if we want to be capitalizing on the new capacities afforded to us by this technology to innovate on those materials, we need to be creating interfaces for designers to manipulate microstructures and composites more easily; to create materials that differentiate for various aesthetic or performance reasons and move us out of the position of picking stock materials off a shelf. We have the capacity now to think of materials as dynamic files. The simple fact that we can now design, draw, and fabricate at higher resolutions is going to enable us to create a new class of materials and, as a result of that, a new class of products. I see a future of drag-and-drop material properties not so different from how we assign digital material now in visualization software.

BECCA McCHAREN, FOUNDER OF CHROMAT

Chromat began as a fun thing to do after work. When I started it full-time, making scaffolding for the body kind of was an exercise in analyzing all the seams and underwire and volume that goes into any dress. It's like thinking about all the structure that goes into regular clothing and then exposing that structure [Figure 1.2].

I love the accessibility [of the Internet] where you can find things that you can have and apply it to yourself. As files for clothing become available online, I really love the idea of being able to hack into a new couture collection and download it and customize it to your own body skin. I see customization as a future in technology and how we relate to object and materialistic things. Total customization.

FIGURE 1.2 Becca McCharen.

That's sort of a beautiful thing because it honors everyone's unique body type. If there's anything in them that they want to highlight, it's possible.

And it doesn't have to be this hierarchy of someone telling you what is cool or what is bothering for you. There's no one dictating your choices except you and I think that's really cool.

To me, globalization is a lot of the sameness. It's sort of like if you're in Spain and you see kids in New York dress a certain way and you want to dress like them. It's like you're assuming that same identity and that's globalization where the New York culture is spreading and everyone's going to assume the New York culture, for example.

But then again, it's like if you're only growing up in Spain or Virginia or wherever and all you see is Virginian people, then having that global influence makes you unique to your specific area but it does make you assimilate to a larger culture [Figure 1.3].

FIGURE 1.3 Adrenalin Dress by Chromat.

There's still craftsmanship because some people can work with the printer better than the others. Some people can follow the design better than others. Like now it's 2015, for 3D printing to be wearable, there's still so much more going into it other than printing that people don't realize. You still have a lot of things to put together. Not everyone can do that. You can't just go home, have zero experience and print something and wear it yet. I think that when people think about 3D printing clothing, in their mind they think of like a fully formed thing that just appears on the printer. There's so much craftsmanship still involved. Maybe in 20 or a hundred years, it will be different. It's like people honestly think that clothing just appears. No one imagines that someone taking two pieces of fabric, pinning them together and sewing them. Even the cheapest stuff that you think appears out of a factory is made by human hands [Figure 1.4].

FIGURE 1.4 Adrenaline Dree by Chromat.

My advice for students that are interested in 3D printing and additive design: something I wish that I was good at is I wish I knew how to work all the software myself. I would really just encourage students to really build their [programming] language skills and then they are in charge of everything. They don't have to rely on other people to produce their ideas. Just be really good with the technology and the software. That's something I wish I was good at.

TYPES OF 3D PRINTING

At the time of writing this book, there are arguably six predominant categories of 3D printing technologies: Extrusion, Granular, Powder Bed, Jet Fusion, Laminated, and Light-Polymerized. Currently, these different technologies enable us to work with a variety of different materials.

Extrusion

Extrusion technologies include Fused Deposition Modeling (FDM) and Electron Beam Freeform Fabrication (EBF3). These technologies have been successfully utilized to print with a wide range of materials: plastics, paper, wood, biomaterials, ceramics, and metal.

Most extrusion processes deposit material on a build plate. The first layer of the print is very important in that it assures adhesion to the build plate and creates a stable foundation for the print. Often, a "raft" is used to ensure adhesion and level the build plate. This raft structure is a platform that is printed before the designed object to help ensure a successful print. Because these prints are built up layer by layer, the geometries must be self-supporting while they are undergoing the build process. If they are not, support structures must be generated for the printing process and removed during post-processing.

These techniques were used at Studio Bitonti in our collaboration with Chromat on the Adrenalin Dress (Figure 1.4). The extruder head was manipulated to give the textile a bias and create a texture that looked more familiar. We saw the extrusion machines as a new kind of digital loom on this project. You will see these again in later chapters.

Granular

Most granular technologies involve a heat source such as a laser, focusing energy to fuse a powder into a solid by melting. This class of technologies includes, but is not limited to, technologies such as: Direct Metal Laser Sintering (DMLS), Electron Beam Melting (EBM), Selective Laser Melting (SLM), Selective heat sintering (SHS), and Selective Laser Sintering (SLS). All of these technologies focus the energy from a laser onto discrete points within a field of granular material and use the heat to melt the material, layer by layer. This process, unlike extrusion, affords technologies more geometric freedom. Materials that have been printed with these processes include various plastics and metals.

Support materials for polymers like nylon are not necessary, allowing you to print structures that are not self-supporting; the excess surrounding powder supports the structure during construction. This will be explained in further detail in Chapter 4 in relation to how complex articulated textile structures are printed, like the 3D printed gown for Dita Von Teese. However, in the case of metal printing, as in DMLS, support structures are still necessary and the limitations are similar to FDM printing. The reason for this is that as the granular powder condenses, it becomes heavier than the surrounding medium and needs to be supported against the build plate. A raft still needs to be employed with DMLS and other metal-printing processes to ensure adhesion to the bed because the metal cools and tends to warp during the printing process. The raft structure will ensure the form does not warp during printing.

Powder Bed

Powder-bed printing has been applied to a wide array of materials; the predominant technology is called Plaster-based 3D Printing (PP). This technology has been used to print a wide array of materials, ranging from the most temporary sugar and starch to the most permanent of materials, including concrete and steel. This technology has also been applied to a wide array of ceramics and wood fibers. Powder-bed printing involves the use of a granular material much like granular technologies. However, what separates these technologies is the binding agent. With powder-bed technologies, a binding chemical is used to fuse the particles together instead of a chemical change initiated by heat. These methods tend to offer a wide range of geometric freedom not requiring any support structures during the build process. However, with many of these technologies, you will often trade off the geometric freedom for less durable parts, depending on what is used as a binding agent.

Jet Fusion

Jet Fusion (also called Fusion Jetting) is a powder-bed technology developed by HP that allows for additional agents to be deposited into the powder, allowing for increased speeds, color, and even conductive materials to be deposited within the same part.

Laminated

Laminated Object Manufacturing (LOM) is a hybrid technology that is both additive and subtractive. This process involves starting with a sheet of material, cutting away the excess, and laminating the cross section to the previous cross section. This technology has been applied to paper and wood and other types of sheet material. It can potentially be applied to a wide range of materials because many of our standard materials today come in sheet form. One of the greatest limitations of this technology is the removal of support materials. Unlike granular processes, where the support material can be dusted away, in the case of these laminated processes, support material tends to be very thick and difficult to break away, making it difficult but, not impossible, to print complex geometries.

Light-Polymerized

Light-polymerized methods include Digital Light Processing (DLP) and Stereolithography (SLA). In both of these technologies, light is used to cure a photosensitive polymer, layer by layer. These technologies are extremely high resolution and capable of fabricating complex geometries, including interlocking parts. This technology requires similar support structures to the kinds we use in the FDM printing processes (extrusion technologies). However, like FDM printing, intelligent design can reduce or eliminate the need for these structures. Materials at this time are limited to photopolymers in a variety of colors and/or degrees of flexibility.

Polyjet printing is another technology that uses photopolymers, but, in reality, it falls into a class of its own. This technology differs greatly from DLP and SLA, in that these two technologies use a bath of photopolymer and cure resin from within the bath. Polyjet technology deposits the photopolymer in micron-sized droplets. One of the great advantages of this technology is the ability to print with more than one material and produce composites also known as "digital materials."

The new landscape of design with computation

The studio I run, Bitonti Studio, is known for using a number of different computational techniques for generating form, producing complex geometry, and using those complex geometries to solve a number of design problems. It is important to note that none of these processes, in and of themselves, are sufficient to resolve any design problem. Instead, these processes are meant to work as an underlying pattern and structure that aid your understanding and approach to resolving your design.

The algorithm is as important as the materials themselves. With the malleability of 3D printing, designers can overcome material shortcomings and embed new material properties within designs. We have seen that microscopic levels of control over materials means that we are able, through geometry, to overcome various material shortcomings most people associate with 3D printed materials.

Use the following definitions and illustrations to act as a point of reference and a primer to get you familiar with how computational geometry is constructed and how you might utilize the patterns that are generated by computational systems in the production of form. This has deep ramifications in the way we conceive an object's materiality, the way we think about customization, and how we approach the design process in general.

Introduction to Computational Geometry terms and definitions

Introduction

Some terms are essential to the understanding of Computational Design. An "algorithm," for instance, is a process or set of instructions meant to be executed in a methodical manner to produce an output. A Graphical User Interface (GUI) is the visual interface through which the user inputs data into a computer algorithm to generate his/her desired output. Finally, a Computer Aided Design (CAD) Program is a program designed to receive input through a GUI in order to render 3D objects on a computer screen. With these terms in mind, we can think of computational design as the process of solving design problems through the creation and execution of an algorithm, whose output can then be rendered on a computer screen using a CAD program.

The following are some key terms and definitions that we will reference throughout the book.

CODE

The process of writing an algorithm for a computer is referred to as Programming, and it starts with Psuedo Code (pseudocode). Psuedocode is an algorithm written in layman terms so that anyone can follow and execute it manually to generate the desired outcome. Once the

Psuedocode is written, the programmer translates it into a syntax structure, or Language, that a computer can read. Some well-known computer languages include Java, Javascript, Python, and C++. Pseudocode that is translated into a computer language is known as Code.

FACE

The "face" of a polygon refers to the solid plane created from vertices and edges of the same polygon. For any polyhedron that does not intersect itself, Euler's equation can be used to calculate the number of faces, vertices, or edges of the shape.

VERTEX

The "vertex" is where two or more edges of a polygon meet. Vertices are often used for object manipulation in CAD programs.

EDGE

The edge of a polygon is the straight line between two vertices. Edge manipulation can create a different effect from vertex manipulation in CAD programs.

TYPES OF POLYGONS

The simplest Euclidean polygon is made of three vertices, three edges, and one face: the triangle. In 3D modeling, triangulation is the most popular way to create any kind of mesh structure.

TEXTURE MAPPING

"Texture mapping" refers to the process of wrapping or tiling 2D images around a 3D model to create visual material qualities (Figure 1.5).

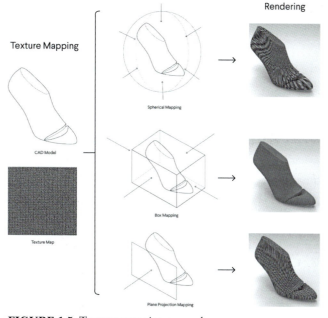

FIGURE 1.5 Texture mapping examples.

RENDERING

Rendering refers to the process of saving an image of a 3D model, taking texture, lighting, and shading into account, in order to put the virtual model into a physical context.

DISCRETE SURFACES AND SMOOTH SURFACES

A "discrete surface" refers to a surface whose edges are formed from the direct connection between its vertices, creating a geometry defined by planar surfaces. On the other hand, a "smooth surface" refers to a mesh whose vertices are run through a mathematical model, such as NURBS

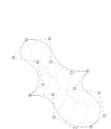

Discrete Surfaces *(increasing divisions)*

Equation Based Surface (NURBS)

FIGURE 1.6 Discrete surfaces and smooth surfaces example.

(Figure 1.6; see p. 107), in order to define an irreducible surface that appears continuous. A discrete surface can never fully generate a smooth surface, however, the more divisions added to a discrete mesh, the higher your resolution becomes and the closer a discrete surface appears to be smooth.

EXTRUSION

Extrusion refers to the process of tracing a geometry along a path or spine to produce a geometry of a higher dimension (Figure 1.7). A curve can be extruded along a spine to form a surface, or a surface can be extruded along a spine to form a volume.

DEVELOPABLE

A "developable" surface can be unwrapped onto a plane. Cones, and cylinders, for example, are considered to be developable surfaces. A consistent feature of developable

Extrusion (along path)

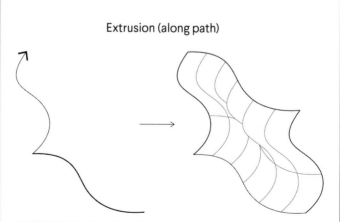

FIGURE 1.7 Developable surface example.

surfaces is that they have at least one flat face that assists unwrapping.

UNDEVELOPABLE

An "undevelopable" surface cannot be unwrapped onto a plane without some level distortion (Figure 1.8). For instance, a sphere cannot be unrolled perfectly with one incision that lets it lay on a flat plane.

Developable vs. Undevelopable Surface

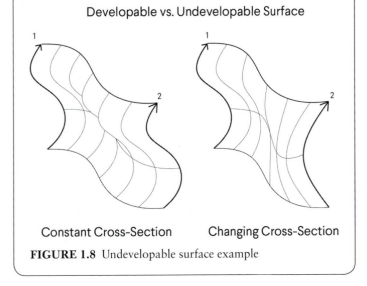

Constant Cross-Section   Changing Cross-Section

FIGURE 1.8 Undevelopable surface example

2

The future of materials

In the previous chapter, we talked briefly about the types of digital and physical technologies available to designers. These technologies enable a completely different approach to materiality than designers have known since the Industrial Revolution. Designers can now play a major part in designing the materials they wish to utilize. With 3D printing, the stock material, or rather the material that one is using as the starting point, is granular and/or discrete in nature. 3D printed materials have no real formal tendencies aside from those associated with how printing services and micro-factories monetize the printing process. Pricing algorithms designed by service providers have traditionally had a profound impact on what 3D printed products look like up to this point, at the time of writing. The landscape of 3D printed goods tend to be lace-like in nature. This aesthetic has emerged mainly due to the fact that most printing companies price prints by material volume, naturally products designed to minimize production costs will tend towards thin, lace-like, redundant structures. Other factors, like print speed and efficient tool path, also play a large role in what influences the form of a 3D printed product.

The economics of efficient form is a very different equation than what it has been in the past. At the moment, the tools we have are not adequate for leveraging all the power the 3D printing has to offer us. Our contemporary design software makes the preconception that materials have consistent cross sections and come in standard sizes. These tools are designed for subtractive methods, where it is much more important to understand the surface of something rather than its volume. Subtractive production methodologies have forced us to put most of our efforts into describing surfaces and not volumes. Traditionally, we carve surfaces from materials where the volume is given. However, for manufacturing in the Information Age, we have different requirements, we need to think about form in a different way. Some designers choose to work around the software and develop their own design tools, or use representational tools designed for medical and entertainment applications. With technologies that can print as fine as 16-micron resolution details, in order to work with 16-micron resolution and represent geometry that is continually differentiating itself at a microscopic scale, there is a need to be able to find different ways of visualizing data sets than what contemporary design software has to offer.

The future of materials will be materials that are continuously differentiating their properties. And this could happen through one material, or composites made with multiple materials, as it is possible to structure geometry at a microscopic level. Microstructures can be introduced that are differentiating: 3D printers do not see any difference between patterns that are repetitive or constantly changing. These differentiated microstructures are enabling us to make composites that transition from something that is flexible in some areas to something that is very rigid at the other end of the spectrum. Also, using multi-material technology, we cannot only control the microstructures but also the relationship between different materials at a micro-scale. For example, if printing with two materials on a PolyJet machine that enables work at a 16-micron resolution, the geometry of the part can be controlled at that scale, which will have implications on how the object behaves. It is also possible to zoom in and operate at a different scale, manipulating material parts of that object and how to transition between those different materials. For example, you might want a smooth gradient or an abrupt transition at a connection where two materials come together. All of these things will have deep ramifications for performance. We can create composites at a microscopic scale that we can control the placement of material with high levels of accuracy through procedural and algorithmic design processes (Figure 2.1).

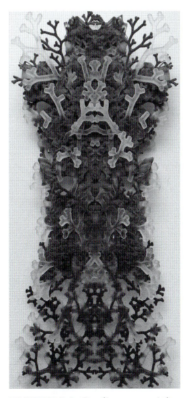

FIGURE 2.1 Gradient material study by Studio Bitonti.

This is not a capability or capacity that human beings have ever had at their disposal before. These tools are augmenting our ability to create and to work with materials and they are bringing about a new class of materials that are going to be continuously differentiated and hyper-specific to different applications and contexts. Materials are not fixed entities, but rather, flexible, procedurally generated systems much closer to data than to how we think about analog materials today.

GROUNDBREAKING TOOLS

At the time of writing this book, there are four developments taking place in the industry that are potentially going to have a profound impact on the development of 3D printed products and greatly influence what designers are able to do with these technologies. They might not be what you expect, specifically because these are mostly software-related problems. Our material future lies largely in the hands of software developers.

1. *Modular printers*: A 3D printer is amazing. It is a machine that can make itself. Why is it that this machine that can generate infinite variability and complexity make exactly the same thing every time it reproduces itself? We will not have one machine to rule them all, modularity and variability are important features commercial printers do not possess right now. 3D printers seem to have encouraged us to rethink every consumer product but 3D printers themselves.

2. *Effective networking and communication between printers*: Shrink the printer down. Get it into the hands of every human on earth. Make them more affordable. These are good ideas, but they need to be connected. What good would desktop computers have been without the Internet?

Distributed manufacturing is a dream that can be a reality, but printers need to be able to talk to each other before we can do anything about it. Every printer on earth needs to be networked. Recently, 3D Hubs reported that their network enabled an average person to reproduce the Statue of Liberty in two weeks. This is an amazing production capacity.

3. *Slicing software*: The way an object is sliced has a lot to do with the way a material behaves, especially with FDM technology. Software that will let us design and engineer new parts and material properties is needed, the order and the way in which material is deposited, the speed, temperature, and infill patterns, all dynamically influence the behavior of the part. The slicer has a lot to do with how the material behaves. People keep asking me about materials because they do not realize materials need to be thought of from the digital perspective now.

For example, developing presets for a slicer or for your export settings is really equally as important as designing the material, as this is what creates the translation from 3-dimensional geometry, which the designer is manipulating, into a physical output. It is the link between a digital asset and a physical asset and this software-driven process creates that very important translation.

The majority of our material problems can be overcome with software.

4. *Volumetric design software*: The CAD software we have to work with currently assumes that materials are consistent all the way through the cross section. This is very effective for subtractive methods of production. If you are carving away at a stock material, you have little opportunity to form the internal organization of the part. However, with additive processes this is not the case, and we can use microstructures to embed new material performance. We

are able to control geometry at very high resolution and build up objects, particle by particle. We cannot design for this condition if we lack the software that will enable us to visualize it. Designers need to be enabled to think about volumes, and not be restricted to surface manipulation.

INTERVIEWS

Andreas Bastian from Autodesk

Andreas Bastian is Autodesk's resident 3D printing scientist. From building an SLS platform in college to producing an angled 3D printer while at Autodesk, Andreas is pushing the limits of what is possible in additive manufacturing (Figure 2.2).

FIGURE 2.2 *Andreas Bastian.*

FORGE [Autodesk's open 3D printing platform] is, chiefly, a robust connective tissue for 3D printers. There's a lot of common problems for 3D printers and there are very few common protocols or ways of comparing apples to apples in 3D printing. There's a lot of human effort being wasted on solving the same problem over and over again. The idea is for FORGE to stick a bunch of engineers who have been working on this stuff for a long time to come up with robust reliable intuitive solutions to them just so people can stop fiddling with these really low-level implementation problems and start focusing on designing with their 3D printer as a tool rather than a source of interesting mechanical problems [Figure 2.3].

Part of [the difficulty of printing fabric] definitely is on the fabrication side [Figure 2.4]. The relationship between the tool and the software used to run the tool. That's one of the wonderful things about 3D printing, because it's kind of working with hardware/software materials electronics; problems in one domain can often be pulled into the more solvent domain where you have

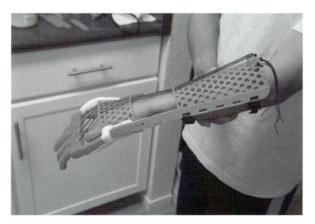

FIGURE 2.3 e-Nable.

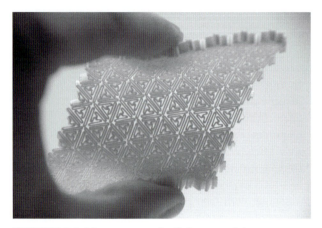

FIGURE 2.4 Mesostructured cellular material.

more skill. Often, problems with desktop 3D printers with electronics, hardware, and material are pulled into the software domain and various tweaks are made into the software like run the extruder cooler or retraction settings are the classic examples. Instead of making a more viscous material, just start with a fine structuring . . . then the printer does the printing.

But it is true that there's a limited set of things that can actually be done on these machines and it's largely just because there's no software to connect the really creative concepts that are beginning to emerge from the design community. There's no software that can capture those concepts. When they first made these machines, they were generalist machines but they started specializing them a little bit more. With all the tool development, I'm beginning to think of software as a tool more now. It's much more sophisticated than the straights and triangles approach. When you think about the classic drafting tools like the T-square and drafting triangles for describing and capturing an idea—you now have much more sophisticated T-squares and triangles that would catch up with capturing the ideas of more complex forms.

Recently, I was traveling, about a year-and-a-half ago, and I was away from my computer, away from my SolidWorks station and I was trying to design a part. I just sat down at my desk and I just said, "Oh, I'm just going to design this really complex 3-dimensional stuff," and sat down and spent six hours trying to design this complex form. So, roughly speaking, it was just a bracket, a piece of the 3D printer that serves one of the measuring purposes. But I found that I really could not convey the information to capture that idea that I had in my head just with pen and paper. It was not only extremely alarming but also kind of satisfying, possibly empowering, knowing that there's this power of the software tool, that it allows you to capture that 3D form.

We need good software to just make it a better experience. It will increase adoption and innovation. Although it's really about solving a lot of these problems that are plaguing the industry as a whole so that people can stop wasting effort and start making more interesting things.

In terms of practically, what FORGE is, it's going to be a cloud-based component of APIs [Application Programming Interface]. A desktop version will support all sorts of data-streaming, data push things and managing free data so it's easier to organize all this stuff. iTunes is good at organizing audio data. iPhoto is good for organizing photo data. What is necessary to organize 3D data in an intuitive easy to navigate way?

One of the things that we started was this information capture infrastructure. So people can start providing feedback about what machines work, what settings work and once we get that kind of communication going, we can really start to steadily increase performance across numerous machine packages.

It's the idea of freeing up that intellectual capital to do more interesting things, to iterate more, to conceive more nuanced definitions of what it is that you are making and ultimately invest more time in designing better than thinking of all those computational things.

Case study: Extrusion Patterning Research

Diving into Fused Deposition Modeling

Fused Deposition Modeling (FDM) extrudes a material, stacking layers, one on top of the other, to build up a three-dimensional form. The experiments outlined in this case study are designed to challenge traditional slicing procedures that tend to rely on stacking 2-dimensional slices. In these experiments, we start to investigate new methods for developing tool paths, transforming graphic representations of tool paths into new material effects. In this case study, we investigate the moment of translation from drawing to material.

In this project, the designers and engineers sought to see if they could design a slicer that would consistently transfer a set of material properties to any arbitrary set of geometries, therefore embedding that material in the translation process from a 3-dimensional CAD geometry into G Code (a set of instructions for the printer).

FDM printing is the predominant technology we see in most desktop printing. One of the defining characteristics of this technology is a woody grain-like texture that comes as a result, not of the machine, but of the slicing technology that imposes a set of consistent cross sections that read as a set of horizontal striations. These experiments had a strong influence on our collaboration with Chromat on the Adrenaline Dress.

These slicing techniques are a product of trying to create material organizations that are self-supporting, this was the most obvious reason but it is not the only reason. As a result, you layer things like plywood and you have ridges along the side of an object. Often, this is seen as a limitation of the technology and an issue of resolution that needs to be overcome. In this experiment, we wanted to test the possibility of developing a slicing procedure that would read in a different way. Possibly it could read as a set of unique material effects, where we are not simply indexing the construction process, but leaving room for alternate interpretations of the object's construction.

Questioning what is possible

What new opportunities does looking at tool-pathing as a three-dimensional operation afford us? For one, we found that it can help structure relationships between each layer of material that might increase the surface area between each layer of filament, as a result increasing the final strength of the part as well as producing material qualities, finishes, and effects that might possibly be more desirable than what we have seen produced by fused deposition modeling, which by today's standards leaves the appearance of a poorly finished part. Could we embrace the additive nature of these technologies to unlock aesthetic potentials in a material that has yet to be explored? For the Adrenaline Dress, we were able to exploit the movement of the tool head to create a digital loom and create a fabric with a bias and orientation (Figure 2.5).

What we found was that, yes, these parts are much stronger. We have created a tool that would allow us not only to

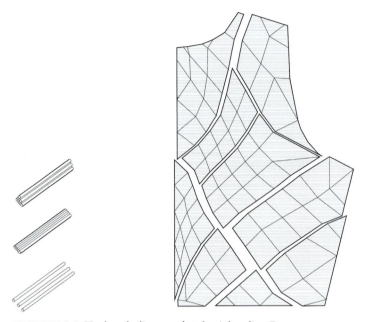

FIGURE 2.5 Tool path diagram for the Adenaline Dress.

consistently apply a material condition across the surface, but also allow us to parametrically differentiate that pattern and exaggerate certain characteristics in different parts of the final object and downplay them in others.

In these experiments, you can see that we replace the horizontal layers with sets of overlapping spirals, which then produce different types of material deposition. By widening or shrinking the size of that spiral, we would create different levels of adhesion, different degrees of softness between the material, and different types of flexibility that we were not achieving previously by using strictly horizontal slicing methods (Figure 2.6). We could also create a gain or material bias to enable stretch and stiffness in different axis.

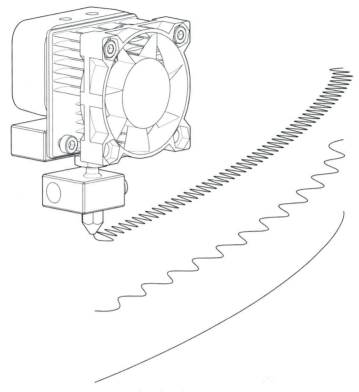

FIGURE 2.6 Diagram of tool paths.

The important thing to note in this example is that we are using the slicing process as a point of interjecting craft. We did not consider the final CAD geometry as the finalized design but rather as an intermediate step, and processed that information into a material construct.

As you can see with many of the images, not only are we able to create material conditions that have aesthetic properties very similar to woven structures, but we can also vary the density or tightness of that weaving across the surface to produce a varying degree of stiffness and flexibility, material structure, and feel.

Case study: Gradient Material Properties

The following project with Stratasys was designed to explore ways of producing continuously differentiating material composites using multi-material printing technology. We used procedurally generated animations of raster images to produce the physical object you see in the photos. We used sequences of raster images to control not only the shape but the material composition. We controlled the distribution of material properties with different color pixels standing in for material deposition, similar to an inkjet printer. In this case, the red pixels are rubber and the white pixels are acrylic; all the different shades of pink represent different combinations of the two. We used an image-processing algorithm to make new material compositions. We found that we were able to create materials capable of continuous differentiation within one assembly. Most important is that these effects are being generated within a digital media that is being controlled and generated by standardized protocol, which can be shared and modified
by anyone.

   This research project was intended for a machine made by Stratasys called the Connex 500. What is unique about this machine is that it lets you print two materials at a time using a photopolymerization method; subsequent models will print two, three, or possibly more materials. It lets you print not only two different colored materials but materials with different mechanical properties. That means you can print something on one end of the object, for example a clear acrylic, and something like black rubber on the other end of the object; as we will see in this example, the material is continuously differentiating, blending from one state to the other. This technology allowed us to print with gradients between both optical and mechanical properties (Figure 2.7).

However, there remains a problem for designers at the time of writing this book. The software the manufacturer distributes with the printer will let you define what they call a "digital material," meaning that you could create hybrid mixtures—combinations of different materials where different durometers are achieved through the implementation of different microstructures. But, crucially, the software does not enable continuous transitions from one material to the other.

This is, in my view, one of the greatest capabilities of the technology and it was left largely unexplored at the

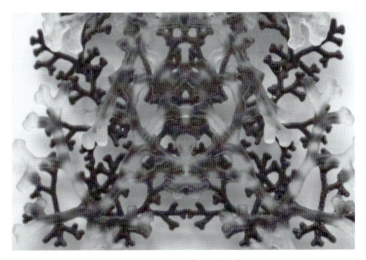

FIGURE 2.7 Multi-material study from Studio Bitoni.

time of writing this book, because users were not enabled to explore that design potential. The software imposed a limitation on potential material innovation. Creating platforms for development is extremely important in enabling innovation in technology. We will start to see, as with other technologies, once there are development platforms that are affordable and intellectually accessible, more and more people will work on innovation in that technology. Rapid development will follow, leading to greater proliferation of that technology and the related techniques, the methods for implementation, and uses for that technology. Ultimately, this is what we want to work towards for early stage adopters of any technology.

To return to the medical imaging example, if we look at the images an MRI produces, we will see different black and white gradients containing different color pixels. Extremely dense matter like bone will be represented as white, dark grays will be fatty tissue, all the way up to black, which would probably be excluded from the spectrum, but everything in between that would be different degrees of density. The imaging software that you would use to read these images then lets you isolate certain thresholds, meaning certain materials of certain properties or densities, and then you can extract from that 3-dimensional model. This is exactly the way we wanted to be able to work with our materials.

The printer was able to deposit two different materials and each pixel represents a material the printer is capable of printing. If you can imagine stacking slices of paper, think of this similarly to an inkjet printer, where you would deposit either support material, a clear acrylic, or a black rubber similar to latex. Each pixel is 16 microns. That means we can, through image manipulation, control extremely high-resolution prints and isolate different material in composite structures from one another (Figure 2.8).

And that is exactly what we did in this project. We used image-processing algorithms to create complex gradients

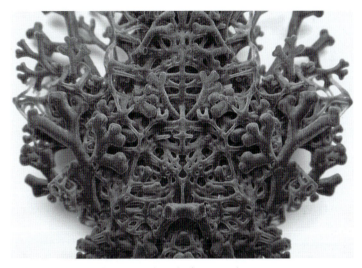

FIGURE 2.8 Multi-material study from Studio Bitoni.

between materials. We modeled each of the structures independently and then our slicer, which writes the translation from CAD geometry to machine code, took each one of those cross sections, applied an image-processing filter to it, and used a set of image masks to preserve the geometry. However, the cross-sectional lines between the material was still blurred, creating smooth transitions from one material to another. The more that we blurred those cross sections, the smoother the gradient transitions that we got in the object. In the accompanying photos of this output, you can see each one with different percentages of blending between materials.

DESCRIPTIVE GEOMETRY

Descriptive geometry is a branch of geometry that CAD programs utilize to generate 2D representations of a 3D object on a computer screen.

DESIGN INTENT + CODE

What is underneath all these different 3D printing processes and digital fabrication technologies is machine code. The machine code feeds a set of coordinates and vectors that tell the tool where to operate or deposit material.

When any CAD file is converted to a 3D printer file, a geometric representation of your design is converted into a set of instructions for a fabrication tool. In this conversion, a lot of data, concerning texture, flexibility, and more, is lost, but the virtual form is successfully translated into the physical world. With the use of computational design, designers are now capable of controlling this conversion, dramatically reducing the divide between what is virtual and what is physical.

BUILDING BLOCKS: POLYGONS

Polygons are the foundation of most CAD programs and scripts that render designs computationally. Many renderings are measured by their polygon count. Too many polygons are difficult to print and expensive for your GPU. Too few polygons, however, result in low-resolution geometries (Figure 2.9).

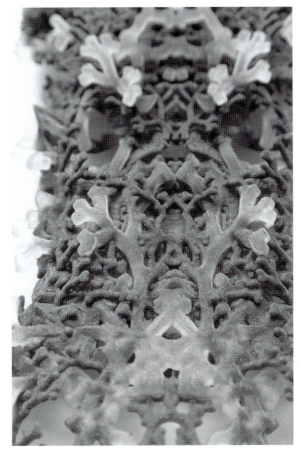

FIGURE 2.9 Multi-material study from Studio Bitoni.

What it allowed us to do, very accurately and very precisely, was create transitions between one durometer and the other and from clear to opaque.

So, why would we want to do this?

This project began because we were designing handbags. We wanted to be able to print things that were flexible, hard, and to be able to control different materials in one place. We wanted to challenge the idea of the "assembly" and create something that was a continuously gradient. One part that would mechanically differentiate itself throughout it's own volume. What we quickly realized is that because of the hard lines between the materials, it became very difficult to construct things like the living hinge and achieve the tactile qualities we were after. Until we considered working with the 3D printer as a digital printer, we realized that we had no reason to think about the bag as an assembly of discrete parts with unique material properties. Instead, we realized that just as you can create differentiation with pixels, voxels can be used to create material differentiation. If you look at the cross sections through this object look like a progression of noise is actually a set of cross sections through what became our living hinge, our first prototype, and what opened our eyes to the possibility of doing really complex material gradients like you see in the photographs.

VOXELS AND PIXELS

Voxels and pixels are digital units used to render everything you interact with on a digital screen. The word "pixel" comes from a combination of "picture" and "element." Pixels are standardly colored or uncolored dots that combine to render a full digital image. When something is pixelated, this is often because the density of pixels used to render an image is too low. The phrase DPI (dots per inch) refers to the pixel density on digital images. The denser the image, the more computationally heavy and clearer it may be. Voxels are the 3D equivalent of pixels. Named from a combination of "volume" and "pixel," a voxel holds information about its location relative to the larger data structure of which it is a part.

This technology gave us very fine control over both material and form, to create a composite that would be very difficult to create otherwise and not with such a level of precision. Here again, we see that we are able to transcend the limits of material by thinking about material design through representation tools used for digital media. We embraced the material as if it were digital media, as we would approach a film or other digital asset. We see materials in the studio being largely driven by data and the structure of that data. We are able to find new and novel material properties that transcend their original intention. If we accept data as our medium, we are able to find and use new material applications and new design and fabrication methodologies.

Case study: Adobe Shoes

Molecule Shoes was a collection of shoes commissioned by Adobe Systems and designed by Studio Bitonti. The concept behind the shoes encompassed a number of things.

One intention was to experiment with multi-material printing. We were printing with three materials at one time. The other exciting part of the project resulted from an experiment to see what we could get from designing the various components of the shoes through an algorithm. We used systems that displayed complex behavior to generate new forms, textures, and color patterns, which we integrated into the design (Figure 2.10).

We used a system called Conway's Game of Life to design these shoes. Conway's Game of Life is a binary algorithm. It operates on a grid and works in two dimensions: the system is a 2-dimensional cellular automata. This means that each cell on the grid looks to its neighboring cells in order to know what the next step is. The algorithm has no global intelligence; each individual element only knows what its closest neighbors

FIGURE 2.10 Francis Bitonti with the Adobe Shoes.

are doing. The complexity in the pattern emerges as a result of these interactions.

CELLULAR AUTOMATA

Cellular automata is famous for rendering Conway's Game of Life, a zero-player game that works through a recursive algorithm. Cellular automata can occur in 1D, 2D, or 3D space, resulting in an array of patterns and dimensional outcomes. In essence, a cellular automaton is a non-linear system that applies rules to a series of cells in a matrix. These cells can either be "on" or "off," often displayed as white or black. The applied algorithm affects each cell and the cells in its neighborhood, creating a recursive system or L-system, where each cell affects and is affected by its environment (Figure 2.11).

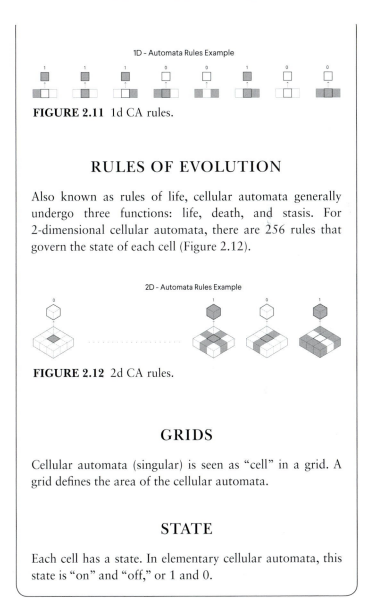

FIGURE 2.11 1d CA rules.

RULES OF EVOLUTION

Also known as rules of life, cellular automata generally undergo three functions: life, death, and stasis. For 2-dimensional cellular automata, there are 256 rules that govern the state of each cell (Figure 2.12).

FIGURE 2.12 2d CA rules.

GRIDS

Cellular automata (singular) is seen as "cell" in a grid. A grid defines the area of the cellular automata.

STATE

Each cell has a state. In elementary cellular automata, this state is "on" and "off," or 1 and 0.

Imagine stacking all of those grids up in space, and then, layer by layer, processing the evolution of this algorithm. That is how we "grew" the heels and platform for the shoe. Each shoe was constructed procedurally. And each shoe was totally unique—we would start with a random initial condition each time in order to generate a new design. We could make as many of these as we wanted, starting from a different initial condition, and each time we would have a different design.

Because of the way the rules were structured, and because they were evolving through time and we were stacking them, the cells would always be connected. Again, if you think of images from an MRI, they are used to create 3D models or they are 3D printing MRIs. We knew we would get certain branching patterns and certain kinds of growth behaviors as a result of this algorithm that would have been a desirable effect, given the structural properties of a woman's high heel. We knew the desired structural patterns were embedded in the system from the start, and this was a good starting point for us.

Another motivation for using this system was that it worked in voxels.

By nature, this is how a 3D printer works. Imagine stacking layers and layers and layers from an inkjet printer in color; then we could start to use this procedure to drive different materials down and/or different colors of materials. The cellular system had a correlation to the printer we were using—both run by square voxels. There were many reasons for choosing this particular system for this project.

If you experiment with these systems yourself, you might notice how different initial conditions play out over time. For example, imagine we started with an oval shape as an initial seed condition. As that grid evolves over time through the algorithm, we would get something that is very periodic, and you would see results similar to a column. It has a kind of static growth and evolution over time, and it keeps repeating back on itself. So, when you put those on top of each other in various layers, you get a column with a repeating texture.

However, when we start with a different initial condition, something that is more random, we would start to see a more complex result. And, in this case, it is something that is branching off from itself. It grows and collides with itself. Some cells die off and then it splits again, so it is compressing, expanding. It is a much more complex behavior and all of this is dictated by whatever initial condition we placed on the grid. You could design your own heels, given a seed condition (Figure 2.13).

FIGURE 2.13 Concept rendering from Studio Bitoni of the Adobe Shoes.

As you can see, this results in widely different outcomes and we have rendered three here.

That is what really drives the form of the shoe. It is what drives the look of the shoe and the style. Our hope is that we could eventually start building applications where users could design their own shoes. Enough constraints would be built into the algorithm so they would not be able to make a non-functioning shoe, but yet they would still have full control and authorship over how the algorithm behaves. The user can almost control it like a game, making it an engaging piece of media that would also accompany the product. You could take this idea a little further and aggregate customers' buying preferences over time and use machine learning to design shoes that customers are most likely to want.

The objective of our investigation was to explore what we could do with color. It was really important to us to do colors in gradients. Until we collaborated with Adobe and produced the shoe, it had not been possible to produce color gradients in solid plastics. You might have seen a lot of these effects achieved in starch-based materials, however, in this project, we used a ridged photopolymer that would be strong enough to support weight.

We used three colors. Traditionally, the way that this machine works is you would have to have individual shells for each one. By shell, I am referring to individual units of geometry. One shell would be red, one shell would be blue, and one shell would be green. When you aggregate all of that together, you would make different colors.

But what if you wanted smooth, continuous gradients? That is a bit more challenging.

To solve this problem, we expanded upon our original research into multi-material printing, where we would blend materials together using images or discrete voxels to represent combinations of various photopolymers with different mechanical properties. (We talked about this in Chapter 1.) We did the same in this project to deposit different polymers that are of different colors in order to produce gradients of color.

This is really what is powerful about this technology. Not only can you print things of different materials all assembled together, but you can also smoothly transition in a gradient from one material to the other. That is what is very unique about this (Figures 2.14 and 2.15).

In this particular shoe style, we made a hard single material construction, but there is no reason that we could not have made smooth transitions between different mechanical

FIGURE 2.14 Concept rendering from Studio Bitoni of the Adobe Shoes.

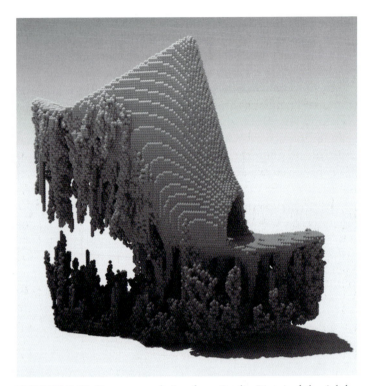

FIGURE 2.15 Concept rendering from Studio Bitoni of the Adobe Shoes.

properties as was illustrated in Chapter 1: different flexibilities, different plastics, different softness, and different hardness— all different kinds of materials. We could start thinking about these things as organic constructions that are continuously differentiating themselves throughout the design.

Ultimately, this product was very important to us in the studio for two reasons. First, it represented the future of customizable products, where users could have a high level of customization beyond just fit. Users are able to interface with the aesthetic and design in a meaningful and interactive way.

Second, it enabled us to think about what multi-material construction *is*. This project was a great way to jumpstart our thinking on that topic.

The shoes represent a future for design, in which all of those multiple functionalities that a shoe design normally needs are isolated and become components that get assembled, folded into one single piece of geometry. I think it is a very unique characteristic.

Voxels are a vital geometric concept for this project; they refer to the most discrete possible element, in terms of resolution, that this printer is capable of rendering. This is the threshold of materials resolution. It cannot print anything in a higher resolution because of the limitations of the tools; the printer cannot express it.

For example, if working with 16 microns as the minimum resolution to represent surfaces that the printer could render physically, we would use stacks of 16-micron boxes. If you imagine using voxels to create the colors of material, imagine how many of those 16-micron boxes you would need to represent a shoe. Imagine them in a 3-dimensional matrix, like a big grid of numbers. Every time you want to print material 1, you enter a 1 into that matrix. If you want to print material 2, you enter a 2 into the matrix; a 3, you enter a 3 into that matrix for material 3.

Now, imagine how images are printed on transparent sheets laid on top of each other. There are different distributions, overlaps, and microstructures. Imagine a high probability of a 1 falling next to a 2 and a high probability of a 3 falling next to a 1 or different kinds of probable mixtures. You could implement more ordered distribution patterns, but, in this case, we used probabilistic distributions in order to print these different materials for a smoother, more organic, and natural-looking gradient. We did not want those patterns and structures to be legible. That was why we tended towards using random functions to distribute different material properties between material groups in most of our projects using multi-material printing. At this point in time, we are researching different ways of achieving these effects in the studio.

The voxels that I talk about when I discuss the discrete units that make up the form of the shoe are different from the voxels that I talk about when I talk about material because we wanted the individual pieces of geometry to be visible. If we treated the growth algorithm from Conway's Game of Life at the 16-micron resolution, generating both material and form at that same time, which is the limit of what the printer could express, we would probably get smooth, sinuous, organic types of forms. However, we wanted to make the aggregation of the individual units visible in the forms as part of the aesthetics, we wanted to express the digital logic that created the items. We chose to make that very visible (Figure 2.16). This was a creative decision.

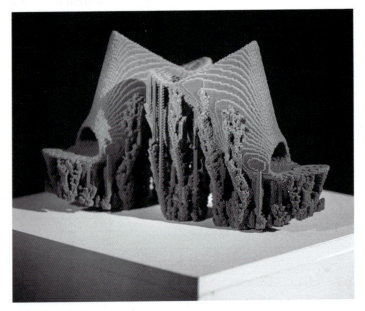

FIGURE 2.16 Adobe Shoes.

Additionally, we used shapes other than squares. We created a field of points, then rendered different kinds of geometry from those points. Instead of using a square as the voxel, we used a tetrahedron, and then that tetrahedron created another type of ornamentation on the surface.

This is another thing a user could customize. If they wanted boxes or spheres, for example, each aggregation of those discrete units would create a different texture on the surface. This project is very much about being able to zoom in and manipulate the product on a variety of scales: from the global shape, over which we have precise control, to what each one of those individual atoms are made of, to how these individual atoms are distributed to create the global form.

From the perspective of design methodology, this is very important because it is similar to Dita's Gown, where we wanted to control the form but we used computation and algorithms to make a lot of different localized decisions about the material.

Earlier in my career, we did not use computation in this way. Instead, we used it as a form-finding method. It was something to drive the global behavior of the form. And if we work all the way back down to the details (in the case of a shoe) can be such that you need greater control of the overall shape and form. In such a case, I like to think of the role of computing in the way we have outlined in this project—as driving material properties, rather than global form and silhouette.

Case study: Gradient mechanical properties in lattice structures

We are looking now to lattice structures as complex assemblies of mechanisms that can be manipulated to produce dynamic material properties that change with condition of use, in much the same way as we did with the above project. Perhaps the most obvious geometric example of this innovation is the graded lattice. Lattices are very useful as a structural and space-filling system. They are used frequently in applications that require lightweight, porous, or structurally flexible solutions. They are naturally present in diamonds, and have applications in construction, aerospace engineering, and biomedical engineering. However, due to its interior porosity, small-scale 3D lattices are not practical for production in a single piece with traditional manufacturing methods. Additive manufacturing, on the other hand, can generate every cell of a lattice within a single print and can therefore control the form and physical properties of each cell seamlessly. In this research, we developed a method for designing and testing graded lattices. Our goal was to design a geometrically graded negative Poisson Ratio lattice that could outperform the Negative Poisson Ratio of any homogeneous lattice with a standard cell structure.

We are focusing these studies on grading lattices to explore the possibility of controlling deformation. Based on our earlier tests, we gained an understanding of the relationship between bend angle and transverse deformation, and how blending between different bend angles can create optimized lattice properties. But the ability to blend between bend angles does not limit us just to negative Poisson Ratios. By blending from positive to negative blend angles, we can do more than just optimize typical deformation behavior.

We can use these techniques to program properties like deflection and stiffness. In the experiments shown in this chapter, we focused on the modulation of the bend angle of a cubic lattice. Based on our 3D lattice tests, we recognized that lower bend angles result in superior Poisson Ratios and higher bend angles result in superior transverse deformation. Therefore, our goal for these graded lattices should be to achieve the Poisson Ratio of a low bend angle lattice and the deformation of a high bend angle lattice. On the graphs shown in Figure 2.17, the

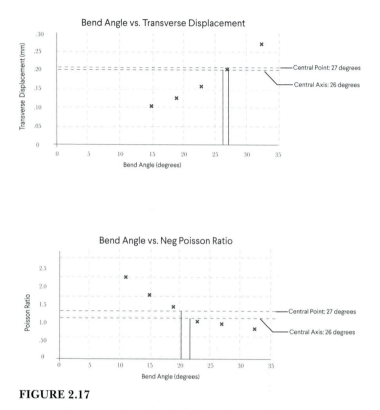

FIGURE 2.17

dotted lines represent how the graded lattices performed, and the resulting lines illustrate what the bend angle of the equivalent homogeneous lattice would be. What our data shows is that by grading the lattices, we managed to achieve the deformation values of a homogeneous lattice with a bend angle of 26 to 27 degrees and the Poisson Ratio of a homogeneous lattice with a bend angle of 20 to 22 degrees. In other words, the overall performance of our graded lattices was superior to any possible homogeneous lattice. More specifically, our central point graded lattice outperformed all the lattices tested.

Looking forward, we are examining how these structures could be used not only to create highly impact resistant surfaces but we could also use these graded geometric structures to make networked sets of mechanisms that both augment and allow the body to take on new characteristics and responses to input forces. We see these structures as networked foams, containing distributed sets of mechanisms that operate as passive exoskeletons or other soft mechanisms.

With the advent of 3D printing, a designer not only has the ability to manufacture homogenous lattices at small scales, but with the blending algorithm described above, he or she now has the ability to optimize lattices for very specific purposes across the entirety of its form.

The significance of being able to create variable lattices is perhaps understated. Lattices act as objects, providing lightweight, porous, space-filling structures that are capable of being engineered for specific uses. However, for a simple lattice made up of an identical unit, it acts as a single homogenous body, incapable of reacting differently along its form. These graded non-homogenous lattices can change in strength and flexibility selectively along their form, depending on the conditions they are exposed to.

A simple example of a lattice family that can be improved upon through blending is negative Poisson Ratio lattices. The Poisson Ration is the ratio of material contraction perpendicular to the axis of strain.

Under tension, most materials stretch outward along the axis in which the force is being applied (axial displacement) and compress inwards perpendicular to the axis in which the force is being applied (transverse displacement). The ratio between their axial displacement and transverse displacement is called the Poisson Ratio.

But, while most materials have a positive Poisson Ratio, meaning they displace inwards perpendicular to the applied tensile force, some materials have a negative Poisson Ratio,

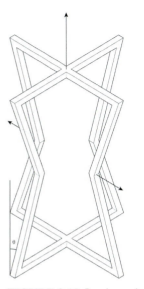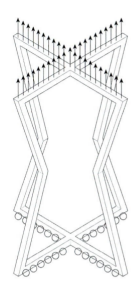

FIGURE 2.18 Lattice unit diagram.

meaning they expand perpendicular to the applied tensile force and displace inward under the same compressive force.

There are lattices with a specific unit geometry, like the one shown in Figure 2.18, that mimic this peculiar property.

The displacement properties of a negative Poisson Ratio lattice, just like any lattice, are heavily dependent on its unit cell geometry. In this case, the lattice's Poisson Ratio and transverse displacement is heavily dependent on the bend angle of the unit cell (also shown above).

The relationship of a unit cell's bend angle and the homogenous lattice's corresponding Poisson Ratio and transverse displacement is shown in the graphs in Figure 2.19.

As the unit cell's bend angle grows, the amount the lattice displaces in the transverse direction grows linearly, but the amount that it displaces in the transverse direction relative to the axial direction shrinks. This creates an "efficiency" problem,

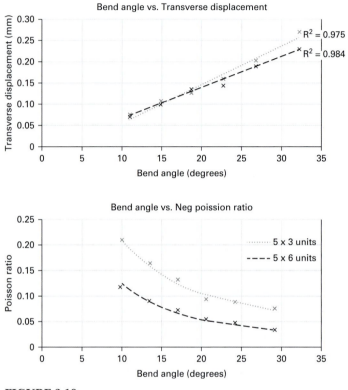

FIGURE 2.19

in that as the bend angle grows, the lattice may expand more, but it stretches out even more than it expands.

But now let us see what happens when the designer creates a non-homogenous bend angle. Using the algorithm explained above, we created two more lattices, whose units blend from a 14.92 degree bend angle in the center to a 32.35 degree bend angle at the edges. The cells of the first non-homogenous lattice blended outwards based on each one's distance from the center

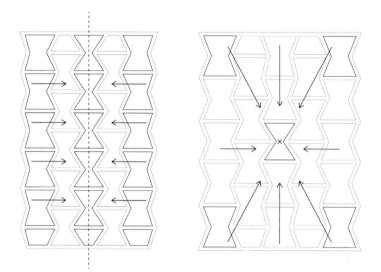

FIGURE 2.20 Lattice assembly diagram.

point, and the cells of the second non-homogenous lattice blended outwards based on each cell's distance from the central axis (Figure 2.20).

Under the same loading conditions, we discovered that both of these lattices outperformed any single homogenous lattice in terms of their transverse displacement and their negative Poisson Ratio (Figure 2.21).

The results of this study showed how the ability to blend lattices at a small scale, thanks to additive manufacturing, may give designers/engineers the ability to optimize porous structures even further. This could have wide-reaching applications.

For instance, with the ability to customize geometry to fit any form and the power to create intricate graded structures at the body scale, designers can take advantage of the strange displacement properties of negative Poisson Ratio lattices to

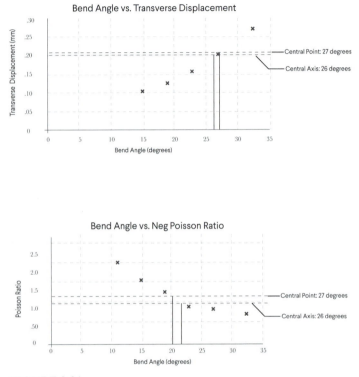

FIGURE 2.21

create impact resistant products such as helmets and body armor.

We have also been working on applications to control displacement, creating targeted areas of displacement within a material. Imagine an orthotic that could apply pressure exactly where you want it when tensioned around your body.

3

Disruptive distribution

As hype began building up around additive manufacturing, excitement led some to the conclusion that we are on the cusp of Industrial Revolution 2. But this is not necessarily the most accurate way to describe it. Or, rather, that this is not the most productive language for designers to use as they approach this medium. Yes, this is similar to the Industrial Revolution in that these technologies affect how we, as a society, form and distribute physical goods. However, in my design practice, I have found it best not to use this language. The Industrial Revolution brought us into the Industrial Age and gave us many new capacities we had not previously enjoyed, for example the large-scale manufacture of goods. I see our moment in time as a time where new technologies like 3D printing and computational design are moving our material world away from the paradigms of industrialization and completing our transformation into the Information Age. I think about the work we do in the studio as designing for the Information Age. I would say it is best we consider changes initiated by 3D printing technologies and computational design as the evolution of our transition into an information-based economy. We are trying to define a design methodology for the Information Age.

We now have the proper tools to interface manufacturing processes with our digital infrastructures that we use for exchanging information. 3D printing is an important piece of an information revolution, however, it is important that we, as designers, remind ourselves that this is an epoch of the informational revolution. We are designing for and manufacturing with the tools of the Information Age. We can observe how manufacturing is being subject now to the infrastructural and cultural changes already brought about by the Internet. Our communication mediums changed how we express ourselves and transformed the desires and demands of brands and a brand's relationship with its customers. If a revolution exists, then it is encapsulated in the fact that we can describe and render physical materials through the exchange of information. It is important that we talk and think about 3D printing and next generation manufacturing within the context of what our existing information-based society has already brought us.

Data has already had a profound effect on businesses. As we are moving into a new era of production, it is important we understand the implications of these technologies and are able to articulate these changes through carefully formed design methodologies (Figures 3.1, 3.2, 3.3, and 3.4).

FIGURE 3.1 Computationally designed jewelry collection for 3D Systems.

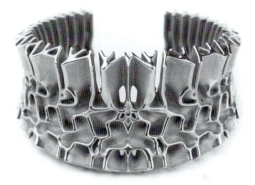

FIGURE 3.2 Computationally designed jewelry collection for 3D Systems.

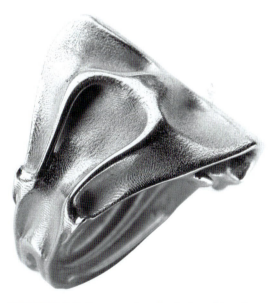

FIGURE 3.3 Computationally designed jewelry collection for 3D Systems.

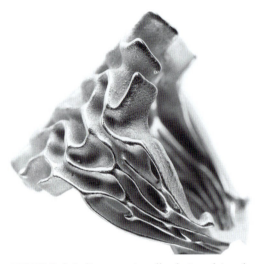

FIGURE 3.4 Computationally designed jewelry collection for 3D Systems.

Will we design?

Many designers describe the first step of their design process as imagining the (insert name of your brand) woman. For example, "I start by imagining the Chanel woman" or "I start by imagining the Louis Vuitton woman." We need to start asking ourselves why so many design methodologies start this way. Beyond the fashion industry, this kind of methodology has very much been appropriated by industrial designers and architects. With the tools we currently have at our disposal, this is an absurd way to approach design. It is necessary that we challenge ways of thinking about products, as both the means of production and capacity to conceive and create are ultimately expanding. Thinking about products as being driven through singular narratives is done in error and is ineffective in our current social and cultural context.

This preconceived approach to solving a problem is a byproduct of the artificial market segmentation that is a symptom of an industrialized world. We need to be thinking about consumers as unique individual data points and not as characters in a narrated work of fiction. Our future is one of continuous differentiation in all respects. As I outlined in the previous chapters, this is one of the key components of the material revolution being brought about by these technologies. As our ability to form matter evolves to take on new capacities, so does our ability for interactions with consumers to take on new, unprecedented characteristics.

Designers create consumers because of the kind of manufacturing infrastructure they have available to them. There is an impulse to create personas and it stems from the need to encourage aspirational purchases through the cultivation of the empathic connections. We do this because we are forced to hold an inventory and engage in manufacturing processes that rely on economies of scale. However, there are other, more powerful, ways to elicit these empathic responses. Nevertheless, with additive manufacturing and algorithmic design methodologies, we can now fold big data into our design methodologies, we can create data landscapes of our customers and use these complex relationships and historical design data and/or simulation to inform our design decisions.

Designers are treated like rock stars because designers are in the business of cultivating deep emotional responses to things. In many instances, you buy something because it triggers an emotional response. This might give the impression that style and trends are very hard to predict. This is not always so and does not need to be the case anymore. This is not true of all industries; you might buy a particular sneaker because it performs better if you are a serious athlete, but largely our response to different brands and products have very much to do with individual and collective identity. Most factors that motivate purchases are not easily quantifiable.

We do not need to keep designing this way. We now have tools and infrastructures that are very good at identifying and leveraging the individual and collective intelligence and creativity of a community. Most consumer brands are heavily embracing social media and different forms of co-creation of promotional content. As we further digitize production and design processes, the reality of community-driven designs and product developments become a not so distant future.

Shapeways, 3D Hubs, and Thingiverse are only a few of the more prominent examples of companies that enable design, manufacturing, and distribution in a digital environment on the Internet. What all of these companies have in common is that they are platforms for creation. They are creative entities that do not rely on a singular creative direction but instead on developing communities of designers and innovators. There is no master designer. Instead there is a focus on distributing tools and producing infrastructure for other people to design and share physical creations.

Let us take some examples from the fashion industry and expand on these ideas. I use this industry as a reference because it was the focus of much of the early work we did at Studio Bitonti and is a stark contrast to what I believe to be the embedded ethos of these technologies. The examples in the above paragraph are very different from how most fashion brands currently run their businesses. They are different because they have to be. Most fashion brands need to have an inventory of goods. Those goods need to change every six months, making the previous season less valuable. The most important part of this is that having an inventory requires your products to be static things. Materials and material constructions are singular static things, incapable of evolving to any particular context. They are not able to respond to a single moment in time the way that information or software can. As a result, fashion brands are forced to be reactive. They compensate for this by very quickly replacing inventories with each seasonal cycle, but the products are the same for six months, no matter what happens in the world. Additive manufacturing can one day afford an infrastructure where designers can start being active and not reactive. We will be able to go to market with the speed and agility of any major media outlet. The fashion industry has already embraced social media in a very big way and it is very good at it. It is very good at interfacing with its customers in a way that allows it to feel like it is being part of the experience of that brand's identity.

Now these sorts of industries are presented with a set of tools that will allow them to expand those interfaces into interfaces for design and product creation. But to do that, they must start to think about products differently, as systems and not as objects, not as static entities but rather as things that are dynamic, customizable, and capable of evolving. Consumers are now able to craft and create their own experiences through a brand. Product customization leads to a better fit; tailoring is a problem that will be easily solved. But providing a better fit alone is not going to give a competitive edge in the future. This is something that is an obstacle now but is likely to be overcome soon and become ubiquitous, a feature of both Brooks Brothers and Walmart. This kind of competitive differentiation will be a symptom of early adopters of these technologies. Building strong communities that operate as an extension of the design department around a company's brand and its technology will be one of the key differentiating factors in our emerging manufacturing landscape. The consumers will need to become an interface for design.

The difference will be made in companies modeling themselves as a platform and not just as a brand, with that very static identity people have to buy into. It does not mean there cannot be an identity or that there will be no more room for the Karl Lagerfelds of the world. The question for brands moving forward now is how to enable people:

enabling communities takes you, as the designer, out of the position of reacting to culture and vernacular design languages, and, rather, puts you in the driver seat to actively create the vernacular. Designers need to think of themselves as participants in and leaders of communities. We need to enable, not dictate.

Creating trends in the digital and physical worlds

Let us look at the aesthetics that surround punk rock music and the punk rock movement. It took a long time for that visual language to work its way to the runways of the fashion industry. To be very specific, a long journey for the safety pin to work its way up from the vernacular into a "high fashion" context. Most fashion designers are always in the position of responding to or reacting to things that are happening in culture, having to work a way through a static six-month inventory; in essence, a reactive response is elicited every six months. As we see the adoption of these technologies play out, one of the most significant value propositions will be the ability to respond to the needs of the customer more quickly and reduce time to market.

If you look at the organic human behaviors on the Internet, such as how memes develop and are shared, these things are able to spread quickly because they can all be created, distributed, and sold in an online environment. For the moment, media needs human beings for replication. Media needs to replicate because if it is not seen and given a context by our processes of communication, it lacks significance and therefore a reason to exist. If you are in the business of creating media, you want your content to replicate as much as possible—this is how you are able to have the attention of your audience. In the age of information-driven manufacturing processes, you are in the business of producing digital media assets.

The goods we consume, like all media, supplement our communication needs. It is one of our many communicative tools. For example, let us look at the safety pin again, which is a very common counterculture adornment that started as part of punk rock fashion and aesthetics. The element came out of a vernacular fashion. They were found objects, utilized partly out of availability and necessity; over time, this became identified with a particular subculture and corresponding set of values. Whatever the context was for that happening, it later started to work itself up the chain; what we would then start seeing is a re-appropriation of that aesthetic in various materials, like safety pins in precious metals. Over time, the goods reach up to high fashion, where that element was later accepted and attractive enough to be adopted by Versace. However, by that time, this do-it-yourself clothing repair had acquired a set of cultural signifiers that made it a very powerful communicative tool that it had utility for creatives working at a very high level.

But that visual language could not have been cultivated within the fashion industry. There are plenty of instances where trends and innovations flow in the other direction. New manufacturing infrastructures and tools will enable new means for appropriating trends and accelerate the rate at which trends emerge and die. 3D printing will help producers of goods go to market faster and with less initial investment. The DIY fashion of punk rock emerged from the appropriation of inexpensive industrially produced objects that could substitute an enclosure or as a means of repairing a torn garment. Innovation was a hack that came from the bottom up.

The safety pin emerged as part of a subculture using readily available DIY resources, produced by industrial means to meet a variety of needs. The ubiquity of the object and repeated

use in a specific cultural context acquired the safety pin new
meaning. The shape was then re-appropriated for "high
fashion" through other materials and production processes,
transcending from subculture to the luxury fashion. The
important thing to note here is that the safety pin acquired its
significance within a medium that enabled rapid replication
and proliferation. Its move to high fashion only happened
after the symbol gained enough significance that it was
then re-appropriated and used as a symbol in a new
context.

Manufacturing platforms such as 3D Hubs and other
community-oriented networks of makers have the ability to
operate in both capacities. They have the ability to be both a
brand and a factory for their customers. Digitally generated
designs are equally susceptible to these kinds of tropes but the
propagation is much more horizontal. For example, I expect
the use of mathematical structures and wireframes as design
tools to become more robust, to increase in heterogeneity,
specifically in the kinds of designs we see propagating through
these communities.

Prototyping technologies like 3D printers becoming
production technologies will accelerate the kinds of community-
driven design activities and exchanges of ideas. If the future of
consumer brands embrace the maker community, then they
embrace their brand as a platform; this filtering-up cycle will
be collapsed into the daily design productivity of any business.
The company is then directly responsible for incubating new
trends rather than being reactive to emerging trends. The tools
of the platform become what enables the community to create.
Further down the line, we will aggregate these behaviors with
machine learning and AIs to further increase the productivities
of these communities. Platforms enable and foster social
behavior. Design is and always has been a social phenomenon
that has very much to do with communicating and eliciting an
emotional response. However, designers no longer need to be

interpreters of trends; they can be enablers and community leaders.

Understanding value when craft and manufacturing converge

To understand what horizontal propagation of trends means for consumer brands, let us start with one of the most significant moments of the Industrial Revolution: Henry Ford's Model T and the assembly line. One could argue that Ford's innovations made something that was once very expensive and only available to a select elite available to the public. At this time, there was a schism between craft and mass production for the first time. To own something that was "crafted" had become a luxury. While everyone could own a car, they could not all have the same kind of car and have access to the same technologies in later years as the automotive industry progressed. The technology available to designers and makers right now can one day potentially eliminate these barriers. Mass customization will bring us a future where we can address our customers as a continuous gradient and not as tiered market segments.

With additive manufacturing, craft and production, or scalable production, are now becoming one in the same. We will soon no longer have a separation between craft production and mass manufacturing. Without that separation, we are going to have to try to find new ways, new consumer experiences, or new methods to communicate value. The people who are going to be the most successful in a future of information-driven manufacturing are going to be the ones who are most active and not reactive in regards to product development. The upper hand will be given to those who build communities and cultivate new social behaviors and norms in order to create new modes of cultural expression, and to being able to respond to trends more quickly.

Materials and the objects made with these materials will need to be thought of as digital assets in much the same way as we think about social media content. Brands need to be as malleable as how we now understand social media platforms. Products should "go viral" by letting consumers interface with the means of production and style. Brands should enable that behavior, not dictate trends. Product customizers should be thought of in the way image filters enable people to take better photos and capture a moment. We need to enable people to capture inspiration as it happens. We are seeing the beginning of this behavior from the companies profiled in this book.

Rethinking IP in a world of digital design

One of the biggest challenges remains of how to deal with intellectual property (IP); how to protect iconic objects and designs while allowing for co-creation or participation in the creation of that object by consumers. One interesting approach is the partnership between Hasbro and Shapeways. Hasbro gave Shapeways a license that allows certain individuals to create objects using Hasbro trademarks or brand specific intellectual property that they have opened up to the Shapeways community.

What is interesting about this partnership is that it highlights a demand for digital trademarked content that can be modified by a community of users. Users want access to content that they already have a connection with and they want to be able to personalize that content. Hasbro loosened their restraint over their intellectual property and gave some of that control back to their consumers. We have seen that happen a lot with open-sourced software and open-sourced hardware, where certain parts of the intellectual property are let go to allow for the community to innovate. This is, however, the first time we have seen that kind of model adopted to a trademarked physical object like a toy or character. Typically, the value of trademarked characters and designed objects such as these is only enforced by the stasis and repetition of the image or icon. It is interesting how for this content to exist in a context or marketplace such as this, the trademark must become editable content that someone can build upon. This highlights the importance of thinking about branded content and a brand's identity differently: not as something that is a shut and closed door. The item is a kit of parts or a template. Designers must begin thinking about what open or loose ends exist and what parts of the product need to be owned by the brand and what parts are free to morph. The future will demand a hybrid model where the customer is going to end up contributing back. For content of this nature it is about designing the points of access and the degrees of freedom. You are designing a space of possibilities and not a static thing. The relationship between consumer and brand is going to be a bidirectional and symbiotic relationship.

This new interaction level might manifest itself in a variety of ways. This is not to suggest that customers are going to design products for companies, but rather communities will emerge around various kinds of content and will begin producing localized behavior, specific to different communities and individuals. We are making enablers of creativity. These assets could begin to differentiate themselves locally, regionally, or topologically through various virtual communities that transcend specific locations, through groups of people who self-assemble around a common interest. This might be from the localized production resulting in different material practices or techniques, or changes to iconography to better relate to different emerging subcultures.

We want to reimagine the role of design in globalization. In an industrial society, you would develop something in a particular part of the world by a particular company with a very particular aesthetic and brand and then you would scale up and distribute that thing around the world—there would not be an opportunity for reinterpretation in a localized context. So, you would have to ignorantly enforce that brand, whether it is alien or not, in that particular contextual location.

If we start thinking about factories as networks of machines largely comprised of consumer-grade desktop 3D printers, and designers and brands as providing content that can be malleable, modified, or manipulated in some way to engage this new medium, then we are facing a world of agile products that are in a state of continuous differentiation. These products might be more aware of a very specific micro-context and different types of solutions. This is the opposite of what was produced by globalization. We are facing a future of global brands and distribution with locally differentiated products (Figures 3.5, 3.6, and 3.7).

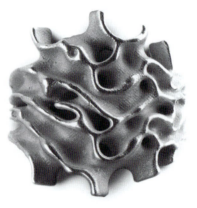

FIGURE 3.5 Computationally designed jewelry collection for 3D Systems.

FIGURE 3.6 Computationally designed jewelry collection for Stilnest.

FIGURE 3.7 Computationally designed jewelry collection for Stilnest.

Piracy in the world of distributed content

Napster had very dramatic effects on the music industry and, later, on film and software. The idea of peer-to-peer sharing enabled the rapid distribution of software and digital music and films. The difference between what we are seeing with 3D printing versus what we have seen with music and films and the other kinds of media is we do not yet have the developed infrastructure for easy distribution. We also lack the uniform medium to make this content valuable. Computers all have speakers and monitors. Digital music and movies have an immediate value. If you download a music file, you can play it on your computer. And then, later, once people were playing a lot of music on their computers, we started getting portable music players like MP3 players, eventually iPods, and then we later migrated into cloud services. Because the piracy could no longer be stopped, sales strategies and entirely new companies developed in order to monetize and distribute that content.

The reason piracy is not a critical problem now is because there are not really enough 3D printers in the world for this to be an issue. I can design something to be 3D printed at home and put it away. But the truth of the matter is that until this technology is ubiquitous, readily accessible, and very easy to use, we are not going to see mass replication of that information, even though physical matter is now in a digital state. We are still in a process of developing production infrastructures to facilitate the replication of that information.

Eventually, software and printing technologies will become sophisticated enough and interfaces will become easy enough to use so that we will have a moment for our material world similar to what we saw with Napster: there was a very rapid mass adoption and mass replication/distribution of a particular kind of data because of sufficient reward with minimal effort.

Another barrier is that, even though scanning technology is becoming increasingly more robust, not everything is designed to be 3D printed. As discussed in the last chapter, 3D printing requires you to understand and design for a very particular material condition that most product designers are not really trained to understand yet. Because of that, we do not have a large percentage of products that can be easily reproduced in 3D printing. However, as designers in any discipline, we should be aware that we are moving towards a future where this is possible.

INTERVIEW WITH DUANN SCOTT FROM SHAPEWAYS

Conducted in spring 2016
Shapeways has provided access to additive manufacturing through an interface that allows consumers to sell, design, and print their own models. This open-sourcing of tools and production also allows mass distribution without intellectual property.

My role as a Designer Evangelist in Shapeways was to find interesting, exciting, and ground-breaking news/cases on 3D printing, help those projects to happen and then help promote them as case studies as to how the industry can move forward. It's like pushing the boundaries and helping to elevate the people who do that work.

There are reasons why fashion is successful in 3D printing. Fashion works on very fast cycles. It's like every season you need something new and people are desperate to be ahead, to be now because if you are not now, then you are not. You don't exist. So these people in fashion are desperate to get into this. I must engage into this now. I must do it like now, now, now.

FIGURE 3.8 Duann Scott.

I've seen the fear of the impact of 3D printing on the fashion industry. It's a fear that they might lose control and I think that it does change control. With clothes, you have to invest upfront in that fabric and hope that it sells, otherwise you are kind of screwed. Whereas, potentially, if we get materials that aren't as fine as fabric, then that goes away. That would mean people are going to take more risks. That means that smaller players can come and play along with larger players. It would just depend on how fast they can print and give it to a consumer when they purchase it.

But it's going to be an adjunct. I mean, cotton's good and there's no way we can synthesize cotton. If we could do that, then it would have happened by now in normal textiles. So I think there's a place for it. There's a place for silk. There's a place for wool. There's a place for synthetics.

The two biggest obstacles in adopting 3D printing in general and in fashion is software and materials. Software is the most important part of design in 3D printing like nothing else. You are currently all just using either animation tools, physics tools, or physical manufacturing tools, and misusing it for a different medium, so that has to change. The second is, material researches have been monopolized under certain patents that has almost completely stopped the growth of the industry. We need to open up and share. The sooner we have that mentality doctored further, then the faster things will grow because the closed patent system is just not helping.

Going back to software, the little complexity that you can do with the traditional CAD packages requires more work because it's designed around machining technical work complexities. We need more ergonomic tools that can be smart for material properties. So, if designing with a material in mind, you have the various tools to build into that. It would fuse sheet-metal tools and SolidWorks. You specify material thickness and type and it would give you the sort of engine you need to do that.

Now we have static single material. Next on the horizon is the "objet machine" and, printing with more complexity still, is the "ICP machine." You can program in different material properties and soon we should be able to make materials that can change. We should be able to put in that it can sense a certain temperature as you put your clothes on so we need to program that into a software as well. So that can make things really interesting.

What you need is the right input. Like the geometry is fine. It's for the structural part of the design. There's no feedback loop. So there's grind-ups against in-graft supports to build. If you make a bracket, it will find out where you want to use the bone structure as much as possible. Things like that. It is about applying a function or a stress or a flexibility so you can say, "I want this grade to flex in this area or this grade of thickness here."

It does the equations on how to make that flexibility and not by manually drawing visual curves and cutting it away and making these patterns manually. It should be about the intent, not the manual process.

Someone will develop it. It just hasn't been doctored upon enough to make it happen.

It would be more interesting as well if you could scan or take a photograph of an object and then file those things and print it up in what file you'd be interested in. Like in a photograph, it would find and recognize that there's 10,000 fields to it and you can choose what order you want it to be. And then you specify from there and it gives you a trio of things and you can print from that.

Or maybe you want to fuse two things, your sunglasses and your phone. You want your sunglasses to be your phone. It's quite a thing.

And it doesn't have to be open-sourced. It just has to be open, in that people can build upon it and monetize it. Open-sourced is great for some things but sometimes it makes a catch. You need to share what you learn but keep some things for your own knowledge.

With design there's a lot of misinformation and confusion about copyrights and patents. Most people are completely unprotected. If they're doing anything, it's like nothing is protected by the whole patent issue. Most people can't afford that. So, perhaps that's why people are scared of sharing what they're doing as they are doing it, because as they are bringing it into the market they get copied or devalued. So, maybe we need to put ways of looking at how we protect intellectual property to make it faster; twenty-five years is too long in the speed of technology. Perhaps we can look at a way of having like a micro-patent in five years to give you a head start or something like that.

I think piracy is funny. It's indicative of where value is at. When there's no piracy of your design, that means there's not enough there for someone to pirate. So, it's an interesting indicator of value. If we start seeing more pirated files on BITart or Pirate Bay, it means that it's worth people hacking onto.

The idea with Shapeways is it's a place to buy and sell products which happen to be 3D printed. It's also a 3D printing service. Now, that's a very important part because there's a lot of volume going towards the service and the amount tends to be different and changes in different times of the year like any retail. It peaks and troughs in different times of the year. But the idea that you can sell a product without taking money off someone, without making it and distributing it without customer service is like a dream situation. It's the ideal if it works. As a value for a young designer or someone who is doing something on the side or testing a product in the market, it's very valuable and really agile.

The thing is, once someone becomes good and established themselves, the brand wouldn't be Shapeways. It's going to be them and they would have owned the consumers and they would have owned the experience and they would have put it in their box. So, as designers come through this system and grow up, they inevitably exit and they do it somewhere else because they can control those things and it becomes their brand. So, it's only for a short period that it's going to be branded in their career. And if you keep it that way, then cross to Shapeways' side, suddenly you come from this beautiful walled-garden experience where everything's brand new, everything's nice, every button's the same, the looking field's all the same, and you take it across to the Shapeways brand—a shopping cart, and it's a jarring experience.

The same thing is true with Etsy as well. To a certain degree, at some point, there's no one who's going to stay

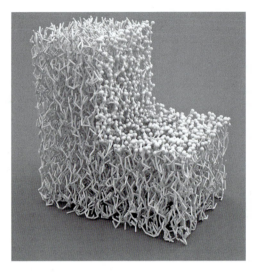

FIGURE 3.9 Bristle chair designed by Studio Bitoni in 2011.

in Etsy. If you become that big, the current modules don't work so well. Then you get out, to control what shoppers buy and control things better and have better reporting tools to run the business. You want more control.

There are certain things similar to structures like Thingiverse, which is just free for all. There's just random things that may or may not print. Then there's something like Shapeways. There's a thing about Thingiverse that is wild. They have moderation based on some ethics at some point. Then there's things like Quirky, in which anyone can consider an idea or something that can get printed up. They get to [a] certain point and if it gets approved, then there's a gatekeeper and that's Quirky. They take it apart and strip it back to scratch and you get no sense of control anymore.

There's Quirky and Thingiverse and then there's Shapeways in the middle, which is where supply meets demand. On Shapeways, if something isn't popular or not wanted, it doesn't get created; it doesn't exist. If it's popular, it gets marketed. If it isn't, then it's nothing. It goes into the nothing file.

The pricing structure on Shapeways was simplified based on the million geometry at that time; the idea was to look at all the files that are uploaded. What's the average density? Figure out a price point of the average one and then apply it to everything so you got a simple pricing structure which is easy to calculate the cost for. It's easy to just look at the file and the volume and know exactly how much it's going to cost. This is fine for some materials but it's not the true representation of the cost of printing. It's an average based on the average. This is how you optimize for 3D printing that structure, by reducing density because you're basically paying a price towards the density scale. So, once you get bigger and reduce the density, then it becomes very cheap.

The problem is the materials are really expensive, so the price point is narrow. What you are paying for right now cannot be reduced that much. And that's based on the material and not on the too many factors that we can distribute. There's not a lot of 3D printers in the US, and Europe have controls of what they charge for using their machines. Until that is broken down, then that will remain. But there's going to [be] more when there's competition. Everything's cheaper when everyone's competing. Material cost is coming down at the moment, so you're not coming from a cartridge, which is cheap and easier to control. We're going to see an awful lot from China or Russia or anywhere they can make their own 3D printing theory. And so that cost is coming down. And then, once we have printers running on pellets rather than filament, that $45/kilogram material is going to come true.

What is interesting and I think what is of value is that complexity and customization are possible, very efficiently. The word "3D printing" is just a word to describe things but it doesn't really matter in the end. It's the fact that you can make these really complex custom things. And whether it's 3D printed or CNC or Waterjet or whatever, it shouldn't matter. The material process should matter. The material shouldn't matter unless the material has amazing properties. It's not about that. It's about that complexity and customization. So, that's like building a business based on doing complex customized things. That's the thing. Building your business based on the word "3D printing" is a bungle.

Divorcing economies of scale

The YouTubes and Facebooks of manufacturing and design have yet to fully emerge, although they are most certainly in the process of emerging. 3D printing will ultimately move design and manufacturing out of its centralized industrial models and into distributed systems for manufacture and consumption. The removal of tooling and/or the rapid design and production of tooling is one capacity the technology affords us that will allow us to make this cultural leap. 3D printing technology is arguably the final step towards this progression into information-driven culture. During the Industrial Revolution, designers moved from working within localized craft guilds into an economy that was obligated to contend with flows of natural resources and capital on a global scale. Manufacturing in the Information Age will still need to engage with a global platform. However, it will be engaging with a new set of tools that will enable more diversity of products and materials than what was enabled by the standardization of modernism.

Prior to industrialization, designers seemingly had a more robust palette of craft practices at their disposal, through which they could imagine the built environment. Post-industrialization, the palette of methods for forming matter was not necessarily limited, but designers had to contend with manufacturing infrastructures dependent on standardization. This had a profound impact on the landscape of manufactured goods. Ushering in the age of modernism was the cultivation of a new aesthetic, one that emerged as designers worked to create forms that would prosper despite the various economic pressures of industrialized production. We see the impact of modernism most greatly today when we see "design" being sold in art galleries. For example, many luxury goods today are a product of craft-based production processes that are not capable of large-scale distribution.

However, production techniques that are inherently localized become scarce in an age of globalization: that need to find audiences and significance in people's lives. This is one of the most significant byproducts of modernism for designers. It forced much of the material and making practices available to designers, and craftsmen, to exist in the realm of luxury goods. This has become not only the place for legacy methods of making, but also for the high-tech and cutting-edge processes that have not yet found a place in common production practices. In numerous ways, industrialized methods of making signify the differentiation between craft and design and the emergence of the designer as a professional. This is why we have the industrial design discipline in design schools today. However, we are now calling those teachings and design methodologies into question. Let us take a look at some real-world examples that illustrate how designers are changing the rules of making and manufacturing.

4

Case studies

Dita's Gown

In the previous chapters, we have studied how the materials revolution and disruptive distribution will contribute to the future of manufacturing and materials. Now let us look at how this all came together in a few concrete examples.

Dita's Gown is a project that I like to talk about when I talk about the future of mass production, rather than in the context of couture (Figure 4.1). The gown may have been considered couture when it was printed, but I think this project is very much looking to a future where every garment manufacturer will have access to these material qualities; these are traditionally qualities that have been limited to couture houses or bespoke tailoring.

One of the interesting things about 3D printing is that it enables an advanced understanding of material—the idea that things can be bespoke, differentiated, complex, custom-tailored, and produced locally. These are all characteristics that are enabled by 3D printing. These are features that will be a part of the language of mass production moving forward, as we start to build a stronger infrastructure for manufacturing 3D printed goods and garments.

This dress was not one of the first 3D printed dresses, but it was one of the first 3D printed garments to be made of differentiated articulated fabric. This fabric is similar to

FIGURE 4.1 Dita Von Teese in
Michael Schmidt 3D Dress. Photograph
by Albert Sanchez.

chainmail. It was flexible; it moved with the body. Dita could
sit down, dance—everything that she normally could do in her
stage wear.

What was also significant about Dita's Gown was that it
was the first time the textile of the garment had been
differentiated to someone's three-dimensional form. Every
inch of it is unique—there is not one repetitive component in
the whole garment. That is because it was generated specifically
for Dita's body from a 3D model. So, not only was the garment
customized, but the actual material properties and the
mechanics of that chainmail fabric were also produced

FIGURE 4.2 Detail from Michael Schmidt 3D Dress. Photograph by Albert Sanchez.

specifically for the shape of this garment. If you zoom in on the chainmail fabric, it looks like a huge diamond grid. There are 3,000 unique mechanical connections on this dress (Figure 4.2).

Dita's Gown started as a collaboration between Francis Bitonti Studio, Michael Schmidt Studio in Los Angeles, the Ace Hotel in New York City, and Shapeways. Swarovski Crystal contributed to the project as well, providing 12,000 crystals to accentuate the fabric.

The project began with some sketches that Michael Schmidt Studios sent to Francis Bitonti Studio. We wanted to create one of the first articulated 3D printed garments. Because of this, it was important to all parties involved that the dress have a mathematical foundation.

One of the first things we had to do was think about how we could create a structure that conformed to a human figure. The human body is a very complex three-dimensional shape. What we found was that it was much more like creating a façade for a building: there are a lot of differentiated components and complex surfaces. And also, much like a façade, the surface had to move and adapt to the form as different forces are exerted on it.

We started with spirals wrapping up around the body, squeezing and stretching over the body like a Chinese finger trap. We then modeled the dress together with Michael Schmidt Studios over Skype. I call this process "digital draping." It is somewhere between automotive and fashion design—you are modeling the surface of the dress as a static object with the understanding that it will become a flexible surface.

Once we completed the silhouette of the dress, the digital draping, we started to zoom in. We started to focus on how the textile would behave. We engineered the textile after we figured out the mass and shape of the dress. We realized we had to produce an algorithm that would allow for us to create a textile that was adaptable, giving us different material properties in the different areas, and changing across the body to respond to the conditions of those areas.

As we designed, one question that came up a lot was: How do we deal with the complexity of 3,000 unique, moving, articulated joints? It was not a simple challenge to manage this complexity, given the material limitations of the printer.

We approached this problem by appropriating a system of tiling. This was the foundation for the algorithm that built up the textile. We knew it would be too computationally intensive to have to go in and build out each one of those hinges, including the jump ring. Instead, we modeled one quarter of the component, then used a system of mirroring, translation, and distortion to match it to the garment. The surfaces for the garment were then discretized. We broke them up into lots of small four-sided shapes over the entire length of the body. We then used each vertex in each of those four-sided shapes in order to figure out the translation.

First, we designed the shape of the garment. Then we designed one of the mechanical connections. When we created the dress, we only prototyped a few mechanical connections. Once we knew that those mechanical connections would work, and once we knew the limit of how small we could go with the material, the rest was just making sure that the procedures that generated the textile would not exceed those limits.

Once all of those components were duplicated to match each polygon on the surface, the polygons were formed by their vertices. Then they were aggregated together and became one seamless textile. This textile was then broken up into parts large enough to fit into the printer—the dress was printed in about 12 different pieces.

We printed the dress in multiple parts on an EOS laser-sintering machine, and assembled it afterwards. This means that the dress was printed, layer by layer, with nylon powder. That powder was brought up into the oven-like chamber and the laser would then go through and melt each subsequent layer, one after the other, until the shape modeled in the computer had been built up. Each little granule of powder is like a pixel. There are very small granules of powder coming together to create a three-dimensional shape, like the voxels that we talked about earlier.

We chose this printing method for a number of reasons. We knew we were going to need interlocking parts in order to make this flexible fabric. Because of those interlocking parts, we knew we were going to need a method of printing that would be self-supporting during the printing process. If we were to use a method like fused deposition modeling (FDM), a process you often see in most desktop printers (at the time of writing this book), we would rely on or need self-supporting geometry. Because we had designed the articulation mechanism to perform a particular type of mechanical behavior—just the way we wanted the fabric to behave—we knew we weren't going to be able to print these with self-supporting geometries without redesigning that mechanism.

We used nylon because it is very strong. When it is thin enough, it is flexible on its own. It is not very brittle. The other reason we chose nylon was because we could dye it. We wanted a deep black, and we knew we would have much more control over the finish and coloring if we could use traditional fabric dyes. In many ways, this was the best material and printing process for what we were trying to achieve, and why we used laser sintering for this dress.

You can see from Figures 4.1 and 4.2 that the dress was excavated, meaning that it was removed from the block of powder. In the photos, you can see the materials are self-supporting, and when it has been excavated and cleaned, it is a fully articulated, flexible fabric.

Surprisingly, the dress is also extremely light. Each one of the components is hollow. Through traditional means of production, it would have been very expensive to have every single one of these custom articulated joints hollowed out in the back, because each one has a unique shape. We would need a specific, unique tool and it would take a hundred hours of labor in order to hollow it out.

However, during the time we produced Dita's Gown, the pricing model for 3D printing was based on the amount of material used. By introducing this complex, varied, hollow chamber on each one of these linear members, we not only made the dress lighter, which was very important, but also helped manage the budget and keep costs low.

With the corset and the crystals adhered to it, the dress weighed only 11 pounds. That is actually 70 percent lighter than what Dita typically wears on stage. Though many people may think this dress is heavy and cumbersome, the truth is it's actually a light, flexible dress.

One of the key factors in designing for 3D printing is that you do not start with the fabric or another material that is given to you. You start with the raw material—and, in the case of Dita's Gown, that raw material was nylon-12 powder. With the malleability and the sculptural quality of nylon-12 powder, it is very important that design thinking begins with the raw materials, not with a yard of fabric.

With Dita's Gown, we broke through this—we did not make a yard of fabric. We designed the dress first, then designed a procedure that would create a material that would be stiff where we wanted support and flexible where we wanted flexibility.

This is a very different way for designers to think about projects, because material property begins to be dependent on geometry. When you are able to manipulate materials at micron level and you do not need to worry about having specific tools to create specific shapes, you can start to think about things in a much more organic way. You can begin to think about how materials might grow and differentiate themselves in nature. These types of material properties and efficiencies are very different from the efficiencies that we experienced in the material world.

The demands and constraints on the designer for 3D printed goods are very different. This dress and the others that will follow are excellent examples of the design methodology that next generation designers will need to move forward.

The Cloud Collection

In 2011, my design studio, Studio Bitonti, launched an experimental shop on our website. We called the project "The Cloud Collection." The intentions behind the project were to explore how an online retail environment might function in the future I have described in this chapter. The idea was to create a product line that could function as a lab so that we could learn what consumer behaviors might be in this environment. The results, as I will outline in the remainder of this chapter, were very successful, showing that the future I have described in this chapter is a not so distant— the tools are all readily available to synthesis such an experience.

When we launched our Cloud Collection, it looked like any other shop at first glance (Figure 4.3).

FIGURE 4.3 Cloud bowl. Photo © Andrew Tingle 2018.

Although this might appear to be like a typical ecommerce site, we are doing something very unique. We have monetized the exchange from data to material. We are monetizing the translation from virtual to physical. Though the press states that the digital file is the point of monetization, it is actually the translation that is responsible for creating value in this project. Once we generated our own customization apps, we collaborated with 3D Hubs in order to create an infrastructure in which these files can be produced.

Due to the shifting nature of materiality and the resulting shift in the nature of production, the Cloud Collection is a speculation on what the future of a brand selling physical consumer-oriented products will look like once this revolution arrives at a time where the DNA of an object is infinitely replicable in the same way that software is. This production model will also expand the capacity for consumers to interact with the narrative around a project. When we produced the Cloud Collection, we made all the products in the collection customizable. We made them reconfigurable. We were not beholden to an inventory. We were able to have an infinite number of variations for a single product because it was not necessary to have those products stored somewhere and distributed.

Every product was made on demand and because they were produced locally, the demand on our factory was distributed geographically. This means that there was not an enormous amount of pressure on any single location to manufacture a high volume of goods. With 3D Hubs, we were able to utilize their network to set us up 76 production locations around the globe—this project was conducted in 2015 and, today, these production facilities number in the tens of thousands. This allows us to create a distributed worldwide web, in which someone could order a design to be produced, where their checkout process involved using their location to connect them with a hub in that specific location. We let each hub set their own price, hoping this would create a self-regulating value for the products.

With 3D Hubs, we built a community around our production, rather than trying to aggregate all the resources and produce in one centralized factory. The consumers were making their own products, using tools and apps that we had designed and they were then sending files out over the distributed network to produce those files locally in their neighborhood. The idea for the Cloud Collection came from trying to solve the problem of selling goods in an information-driven manufacturing environment.

When we are looking at the 3D printing industry, we are seeing that printer manufacturers are moving towards producing less expensive consumer-oriented machines by the market. If we look forward at what will happen if those machines start to saturate the market, we are going to end up with a series of micro-factories, which will result in a global manufacturing landscape of small-production facilities or people printing objects or products at home. Taking a step back, and looking at that scenario coupled with the fact that we can describe objects digitally, the tools for engineering or reverse engineering a digital file into a material reality are going to become more readily available. Users will be able to manipulate digital media to exhibit the kinds of material properties and performance they expect from physical goods through computation. How are we going to deal with this new landscape, in which physical matter and the digital environment are colliding?

That was the question that we were trying to speculate on and solve with the Cloud Collection. We were looking at the future of manufacturing. Specifically, what it will mean to manufacture goods and provide content to an infrastructure of consumer-grade technologies that are going to be more capable than the most powerful factories in the industrialized world. 3D Hubs released some statistics in 2011, in which they said that at the time when the statistics was released, they had about 6,000 printers in their network. That network was capable of producing enough material if someone wanted to, to print all the parts of the Statue of Liberty in a week and a half. That is an amazingly significant production power that most people have access to. Certainly, the liberation of such a production capacity marks a major step in human evolution.

3D Hubs is able to do that because they have distributed the production power and they are taking advantage of idle times of machines from around the world. Not that different to how we think about computing today. We spread computing or intense computations out over many Central Processing Units (CPUs—"nodes" are used here as reference to production machines or individuals in a network) in order to increase the efficiency in the computations that enable us to do more. It is very important that we think about manufacturing for the future as a distributed paradigm; something that is cooperating at a global scale through a series of network nodes.

After a design is released from the app to the manufacturing hub, the design is released under a creative commons license. We do this because our point of monetization is at the interface where the customer can create a digital design and convert it from a digital file into instructions for the machine. They are able to create something physical that can be produced through any manufacturing hub they choose. What the customer does with that digital file we are not concerned with. We are concerned only with providing design tools and digital content that the user can then convert into something physical.

In designing the infrastructure for this project, we saw our opportunities for producing revenue were where the file was made or designed, and then at the intersection where it was switched over into a physical object and fabricated. We were relatively unconcerned with what happened to the design in between those two phases and thus we decided to release all designs produced by our app under a creative commons license. There was no reason to restrict the intellectual property or prevent intervention or replication from the customer at that phase of the transaction. We only wanted to be sure attribution was provided, that was all that was necessary post-transaction from the app.

As a brand, we want ubiquity and people seeing and using our products, but we also want to make sure the brand is associated with enabling the creation of that content. We did not really have any second thoughts about releasing all of those digital files under the creative commons license, especially since we see the content as being co-created through the app. In a way, we are producing design software. We observed that it enabled for that product to be customized; if worked along with the consumer to shape it in that particular way, it would lead to evolutions of the design we could not have expected to make ourselves in the studio.

I would like to return to the idea of designing specifically for 3D printing as a unique material condition. There is importance in starting to expel the myth that it is a technology that will just make anything. On some level, that is true. Some printing technologies are much more flexible than others. Materials that are 3D printed have their own material qualities that are very different when compared to materials that have a consistent or predictable cross section. In the case of the Cloud Collection, we were designing using a desktop fused deposition technology, which is an extrusion technology. You are building up layers of material, layer by layer. It was very important to us that there was no post-processing needed. These objects may have been made by a professional hub or made by somebody at home. If somebody at home made it, we could not expect them to do something beyond turning the printer on and loading a file. That is why we needed to build with very specific design considerations: the designs were to be printed on FDM technology, thus a lot of work was done in order to ensure that all the files produced by our systems would be self-supporting structures that did not require support material. It was important that the print did not need to have support materials removed. It did not have to be sanded, tumbled, or painted. The parts that we would get from the printer needed a very clean, glossy finish right off the printer so anyone could just literally pull the finished object directly without human intervention or post-editing.

When we designed the software interface to help the customer customize the products in the Cloud Collection, we chose to constrain the levels of customization quite a bit. We did that because it was very important to us that we were curating the interactive experience as well as enabling participation in the creation of the product. We did not want them to spend a lot of time designing an object, but we also wanted them to feel like they had enough authorship or ownership of their design to call it their own.

FIGURE 4.4 Cloud. Photo © Andrew Tingle 2018.

The idea was that we would build the narrative of a product around the idea of entropy; the designs were built around the idea of eroding away a solid. We gave users only enough control in the interface to allow them to participate in that narrative of degradation: introducing holes and therefore more complexity. These very intricate branching patterns would be exposed, depending on how much or how little spatial complexity was introduced into their system.

What we found with that was that consumers started to develop very particular behaviors when customizing these products versus other products; it was not that they did not know what to do, they very quickly started to pick up on the design intent that we embedded into the behavior of the software. For example, producing things in series or serials— we would very often observe consumer behavior where somebody would purchase one on the far end of the spectrum, another would purchase in the middle, and another on the opposite end of the spectrum.

Because what they saw was a narrative in the app interface, that translated itself into the product, which influenced their purchasing behavior. Even though they were capable of continually differentiating the design, we found that because of the restrictions in what they were able to customize, there was a kind of narrative that was more or less commonly shared amongst all the users. We could then see the narrative translate into the buying patterns of our customers.

This project is also an amazing opportunity to talk about the future of craft relative to a model of production like this. A lot of people see the patterns or the kinds of geometry that we are able to fabricate in the studio. And, most often, they find themselves baffled or wondering how it was done. For example, when I released the Cloud Collection, I got an email from a

FIGURE 4.5 Cloud. Photo © Andrew Tingle 2018.

customer who was watching the print and noticed a steep overhang without support material. In his email, he was assuming something was wrong with the system and this could not be right. I told him to wait it out and that it would be fine. Later that day, I got an email saying he was shocked that it printed beautifully.

The reason for this is because we do not use traditional CAD software. Most often, you would see this kind of variation happen through using a parametric model, meaning very simplistic relational sets of parameters. A parametric model is a set of relationships; we will discuss these types of systems in depth in the next chapter. For example, the radius of one end of the vases would be linked to the radius in the middle. So, if I scale the middle, we might start to see some different changes cascade. The problem with these kinds of methodologies is that they tend to be somewhat linear. Inherently as you are going through a customizer, the variants that you are getting are expected. We are not able to break topology, adding holes and other complex transformations. We are not able to go, for example, from a shirt to a pair of pants.

CREATING CURVES

So far, we have looked at polygons and shapes with straight edges. While these rigid forms are building blocks, Bezier curves, surfaces and triangles allow us to step out of the linear world and into one of elegant and natural-looking structures. Looking at curved surfaces also introduces us to a popular type of 3D modeling, NURB-based modeling.

NURBS

Non-Uniform Rational B-Splines, also known as NURBs, create curved surfaces in 3D modeling through a series of control points, which define Bezier curves that are then connected together to form a NURB-based surface.

Control Points

Control points are simply two locations between which a Bezier curve can be located. Translating control points causes the Bezier curve to recalculate as control points act as a "link" from one curve to the next. The curve aims to link to the next curve at a 180 degree angle at the control point.

Bezier Curves // Mathematical Freeform Curves and Surfaces

Bezier curves are curved segments between control points that link together to create a path. In both 3D modeling and vector-based design programs, paths can be easily manipulated and scaled for smooth, curved geometries.

Bezier Surfaces and Bezier Triangles

Creating curved surfaces is done well by Bezier meshes, which are generated from a series of Bezier triangles. Bezier triangles are Euclidean triangles that can have curved edges and are not required to be planar, allowing them to pass into three dimensions while still having one face.

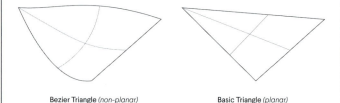

Bezier Triangle *(non-planar)*   Basic Triangle *(planar)*

FIGURE 4.6 Triangle and surface example.

Splines

Mathematical splines are the foundation for curve-based modeling.

A spline is made up of a series of polynomial functions that connect at knots. These knots are the basis for control points we use today on Bezier curves and in NURB-based modeling. Polynomial functions aim to have high continuity at each knot, meaning the function curves smoothly to create a 180 degree angle, where it meets with the next polynomial function. This is what creates the smooth, curved shape that we identify with NURB-based modeling.

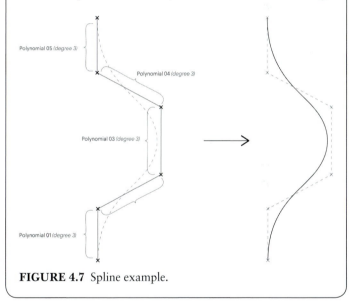

FIGURE 4.7 Spline example.

We tried to break that on this project. In the studio we tend to think through algorithms that have nonlinear behavior. This is why, very often, especially in our customizers, we are able to generate such a wide range of variations that all look very different from each other. In the Cloud Collection, at the far end of the spectrum, it might look like something that was pulled off of a tree. From the other far end of the spectrum, it looks like a very primitive clay bowl or clay vase or something that might seem to have absolutely zero articulation. The reason for that is because our studio has been dedicated to using systems that have some kind of embedded intelligence in them, which are capable of creating structures that might be beyond our expectations of how systems behave or how we are used to seeing industrial or mechanical systems behave.

I think this is a very important point because, moving forward, it is what enabled us to deal with so much complexity, what enabled us to have 30,000 unique mechanical parts on a dress or, in the case of the Cloud Collection, thousands of unique angles. All of which are capable of being self-supporting and printed on a desktop printer. It is because we are able to build constraints into complex systems that generate form. We are able to give them very simple, basic rules, needed to control material output or to ensure certain quality of material output when engaged in designing for co-creation platforms dependant on distributed manufacturing models. But, at the same time, it transcends traditional common restrictions that are associated with the way we think about geometry and how we think about constructing geometry, which has largely been dictated by a Euclidian understanding of the world (Figure 4.8).

What this does is put the designer in a position where craft, and producing emotional responses to objects really becomes about our ability to creatively manipulate large sets of data. And not only manipulate them, but put them in a digital context, in which they are capable of cultivating unique structures and behavior while being reactive to users' demands. And this is going to be, in the future, the source of material innovation. This future of material innovation is going to come

FIGURE 4.8 Cloud. Photo © Andrew Tingle 2018.

from people who are most skilled at manipulating large datasets for aesthetic and performance-driven material fabrications.

How does one remain competitive in this market?

We already know how to deal with this. We already know how to use and manage open-sourced software. This is something that is very new for people who are producing material goods. But what we are moving towards is a condition in which material production and material innovation is going to be largely cultivated by our manipulation of software, our being able to manipulate software and information and data in culturally meaningful and socially relevant ways.

What does this mean in a larger context for brands and designers?

It is tempting to turn this discussion to Internet memes. We are moving into markets that are going to be largely guided by social interaction in digital space or non-physical space. Social networks have become the public spaces. They have become the parks and town squares of our generation. Grabbing attention in these spaces is the key to social proliferation of any content.

If we look at successful memes, they perpetuate themselves because they find themselves the fastest route through emotional responses. This is very similar to various products, in that purchases in this space are led by those who are able to trigger emotional responses in a way that other goods cannot. Traditionally, this has been a very difficult practice, which is why it has always been an industry where designers play such an important role; in order to really maximize the percentage of the market that you are able to take, you need to be producing within your market segment the most of these kinds of interactions.

The relation to Internet memes is that they are social constructs and/or creative constructs that are very good at replicating themselves in a digital environment. It is a creation of a piece of culture that is then shareable and easily modified. Makers either already put their creative stamp on it, or they trigger an emotional response in someone, who then wants to share that emotional response with somebody else.

When we look at the kinds of apps or software that have emerged around that type of social phenomenon, we notice an emergence of a meme that is usually related to some sort of a cultural moment, film, music, something in the news. It starts to populate, and then things start to emerge or products start to emerge or apps start to enable the cultivation of that meme. This all still starts with something external. Brands and designers are not exempt from producing that spark, but they need to ensure that they provide their audience with adequate tools for rapid replication and modification of that media.

CONSUMERS TAKING OWNERSHIP OF PRODUCT DESIGN

Our objectives in the future are going to be attempting to create content that is able to go viral. This is why we released all our files under the creative commons license for the Cloud Collection. We wanted to encourage people to modify and replicate the design. The more prominence the object has in the virtual space and is digitally replicated, the more likely it is to be physically replicated, which is our end goal. Viral content is going to enable market dominance despite wanting to divorce ourselves from that, as designers, as most designers consider themselves artists capable of creating their own sort of unique world and unique view. We need to figure out how we can be much more sensitive to social conditions, producing platforms that enable people to participate in different modes of culture. It might mean cultivating modes of culture; essentially, what we are producing are little snippets of software that are actually like meme generators. We are allowing for the proliferation of a very particular cultural artifact that is a direct product of a specific brand's identity.

For example, another very interesting thing about the Cloud Collection was that after we launched, people started doing things with our products that we did not think of ourselves, and they were sharing them on social media. For instance, one person actually cast one of their items in ceramic. Somebody else used a spray-on metal coating and was making metal versions of the product. There was a very interesting surfacing of a secondary community of people who are not really just passively consuming these objects, but, rather, actively engaging with them and building on them and teaching us new things that we could be doing with our materials, our processes, and our platforms.

This was very good for us in a number of ways. On one level, we were learning from the community. The community was feeling as though they were engaged with us. Through the feeling of engagement or enabling of creation, we were cultivating the desire to share in other people. We were linked to that. It actually became really good marketing and material research for us. Our customers were distributing our product for us and conducting new fabrication research for us.

While on the software side we may have restricted the user a little bit more than most other customizers did, there was still a wild proliferation of people adapting or engaging in new material practices that we had not anticipated through each one of these manufacturing hubs (Figures 4.9, 4.10, 4.11, and 4.12).

FIGURE 4.9 Cloud. Photo © Andrew Tingle 2018.

FIGURE 4.10 Cloud. Photo © Andrew Tingle 2018.

FIGURE 4.11 Cloud. Photo © Andrew Tingle 2018.

FIGURE 4.12 Cloud. Photo © Andrew Tingle 2018.

INTERVIEW WITH BRAM DE ZWART
OF 3D HUBS

3D Hubs is a network of 3D printer owners around the globe. Through allowing these early adapters to turn their living rooms into production stations, the concept of a micro-factory is becoming a reality.

I think it started about seven years ago, when I studied industrial design. I had a Master of Science in Industrial Design and learned everything about how to set up large-scale production in China and developing products for them. In my free time, not a part of my curriculum, I learned about 3D printing and I was so amazed when I realized that the whole model that I was taught to execute on could be disrupted. Instead of making stuff far away in China, we can make it very close to the end-user. That we would make products on-demand instead of having

FIGURE 4.13 Bram de Zwart.

to do years of development and setting up production and these products could be personalized so it wouldn't be identical.

After graduating, I worked at Freedom of Creation, which then got acquired by 3D Systems. Around that time, I was sitting in bars with Brian, obviously [Brian Garret, co-founder of 3D Hubs]. He was my colleague, with the same sense of calling and inspiration. To us, well-known 3D printer suppliers producing and supplying from only one location, even if the customers are on the other end of the planet, didn't make sense. We started thinking how can we change that. We didn't have a lot of money. We just started figuring out how we could start some simple platform together, where we could access all the idle 3D printers out there through an online platform, and we wouldn't have to buy the 3D printers. We just could use it at idle times. Why won't they monetize that?

That's how 3D Hubs started. We basically spent, like for almost a year on it, every evening and weekends while we were still working at 3D Systems. But at some point, you get so engulfed about the idea and say, "Okay, we want to do this full-time." So, we decided to do it and we got permission from the CEO of 3D Systems to actually start doing it.

There are people saying we should mark a place first, like free liquidity in a certain geographic region, and then once you know all the strings you have to pull in order to create liquidity, then you can copy that to different cities. We were aware of those theories. We just didn't know why things would stop at a border. With the Internet and with 3D printers being everywhere, let's just go global. Ultimately, our goal is to give people access to 3D printing as close to your home as possible, so why limit it to one city or one country?

We hope that our brand eventually becomes a movement. It's a pretty big word, "movement," but I really hope that being a part of the movement is the consensus because we're definitely not the only ones who find joy in changing the way to design, manufacture and distribute products.

When we started the company, we first thought of it as very transactional. We just enabled people a place to 3D printshop with a local service provider. They go through a platform and we take a commission on the order and that's it. That's our company.

I see the designer more of a facilitator of users to bring out more creativity and bring out cool designs and give them the feeling that they did it all themselves. It means that the designer will be put less in the spotlight and have a more modest role instead. I think it will work best if people who are not designers are feeling that they created something very cool. That means that we need smart designers who think, "How can I be able to facilitate them to do that?"

For 3D Hubs, let's say, right now, we just enabled companies and individuals to get their 3D prints made a lot faster and more affordable and they actually get to see the 3D printing process. That's what we're enabling. That means that we're making 3D printing more accessible and a more viable option compared to traditional methods. So that's the first step. The next step is getting the companies that have the most influence with larger crowds in the general public to also get excited with what 3D printing enables, what it allows them to do. It allows them to engage their users more.

For me, there are three benefits of 3D printing. The fact that you can manufacture locally. The fact that you can manufacture on demand. The fact that you can personalize. You have a lot of design freedom. Of course, there are more benefits but, for me, these are the three that are on the top of my list. One negative implication would be we're creating a lot of waste, right? Everyone gets access to production and everyone starts designing, there's a risk that products get disposed of much faster.

And yet, I think 3D printing and other technologies are part of a change where we look for more local communities. I hope 3D printing gets us to where we move towards a future, where we become more independent. We're creating a bunch of local communities who grow their own foods, their own electricity, their own products using solar cells, wind power … more efficient ways to growing our foods and 3D printing may enable that … It's a very long-term objective.

It's in a book by Lionel Robbins. It's somewhere. I've read it. He said that technologies like 3D printing will free the world in a few decades because there will be abundance so no one will work. I think the 3D community is really helping to democratize manufacturing so you might call it a movement now. Karl Marx said, "Power is in the hands of people that owns production."

INTERVIEW WITH BRE PETTIS FROM MAKERBOT

Makerbot is one of the most familiar names in the home 3D printing space. The Replicator 1 and 2 have become a standard for home extrusion machines and Makerbot's filament innovation is leading the way while providing a centralized location to purchase new plastics.

Makerbot's mission is to empower everyone to make anything. We did a pretty good job of actually bringing awareness to 3D printing. When I started, nobody knew about it and I wanted one because I couldn't afford one.

Now, with Bold Machines [an independent product development workshop], our goal is to show people what you can do with it. We're partnering with all sorts of folks to empower them with technology and we got the firepower here of all the Stratasys 3D Printers. From the wax 3D printers, we're getting Apollo jet 3D printers, which are multi-color, multi-material. Then we've got a legion of Makerbots and access to Stratasys 3D printers.

We're working with people in the furniture industry and the fashion industry, people in the design industry. The whole goal is to basically say, "Hey listen. You could take ten years to adopt this into your practice and that

FIGURE 4.14 Bre Pettis.

would be the natural course of events or we can jumpstart you ten years into the future and get the show on the road now and you can be a leader."

It has never been a better time in the world to be a creative explorer. It's just fantastic. If you want to make something, the tools are accessible, the software is getting easier to use and if you want to integrate electronics, those are modular. If you want to add software, there's so many examples that you can use as a framework to get started with. The game is really on.

It used to be that in order to make really cool stuff, you basically had to be a tycoon with access to a factory. Now, you just need to have a laptop and access to a Makerbot and a sewing machine.

It's similar to when desktop publishing started to happen, when blogging started to happen. We're seeing the democratization of everything where it used to be a very centralized production. Now, it can be decentralized. You can be an individual person and utilize the resources of the world and have an empire but it's just you.

The biggest impact that 3D printing has in industry is that it compresses the innovation cycle. It used to be that if you wanted to make something, you would design it and you probably would need to hire somebody to do it in CAD and translate your drawings into CAD. Now, you can just do it yourself in CAD. It used to be that you are descended off and it would take weeks or months to do a revision, to do an iteration and that's called rapid prototyping.

When you have a Makerbot in your desktop, it's not even rapid anymore. It's real-time because you're making something and as it's being made in front of your eyes, you're like, "Oh! Gotta change that," and you're back into the design changing it. By the time your iteration is done, you got another iteration ready to go. This ability to iterate just makes failure a part of the process rather than a showstopper. You can prototype your models. You can prototype your ideas. You can do an iteration and you don't have to stress out if it isn't perfect. That kind of shift in mind frame is probably the most important thing going on right now.

Makerbot's Thingiverse is a site that empowers people to share things and download things for free, with the goal of mutual co-arising: very powerful. I think different people use Thingiverse for different things. For a lot of people, it's their passion. It's their hobby. They make things. They share it. They love seeing the iteration. They love seeing things evolve. They love seeing people make stuff. That's what I use it for. It makes me happy. When I see emerging artists and what they'll do—they'll put some of their work up there and it's mind-blowing. It allows every 3D printer in the world, not just Makerbots, to be a portal for their artwork to enter the world.

It's a whole new world that we are exploring and I think we just started exploring it, just to the beginning of the frontier of what an openly shared community like Thingiverse can do.

So there's that and then there's the Bitonti crazy dress that anyone can make. Being open, sharing everything— you're getting the benefit of making this amazing work and you don't have to rely on cheap labour in Bangladesh to make it for you. You're just saying, "Can everybody else please make this?" It's so unique, so iconic that your name has to be associated to it when people explain, "This is a Bitonti dress." Then you're just totally messing with the system.

I have a jacket project that I'm working on where it's a Tyvek jacket. Tyvek is a material I've always wanted to work with. It's the stuff you cover houses with before you put siding on it. We're making a Tyvek windbreaker and the print on it is like an STL mesh. It will have triangles all over it and it will make you look like an STL file. It's a project I'm doing with Betabrand.

3D printing garments is a constraint. Garments want to be fluid and flexible. Plastic is not naturally fluid and flexible. But these are the challenges that bring about genius. You look at the Eames couple. They are like, "Okay. We've figured out how to bend plywood. How to make plywood in bended curly shapes." And they're like, "Let's make furniture." They learned how to do it by making propellers for the military. And they're like, "This is a cool kind of process. Let's extrapolate this to furniture and do all the cool stuff you could possibly do with this." And they just did it. They created a body of work and they've basically owned the brand of bent plywood.

Totally bad ass, right? If you think back to it, it's pretty obvious. Bent plywood makes furniture. Super obvious for us in retrospect but at that time, it must have been: "Okay. We can bend this so that means we can attach things to different parts but we need to use rubber grommets. That's never been done before. Where do we get these things?" It's a real challenge. They took on a real challenge and they came up with an amazing response.

3D printed garments is a similar challenge. You can't make fabric out of a 3D printer yet, but you can make something that looks more like chainmail. This sort of challenge of making things out of plastics that are hard to go on the body, we've only seen the beginning. We've seen shoes. We've seen accessories. We've seen hats. We've seen whatever those things that stick in the front of people's heads. My instinct is that somebody is going to come around, take the design challenge: "Okay. It's gonna use armor as a model." Use sort of like bondage as a model where things have to be tied on. There's an element of attaching things and an unlimited palette. I'd like to see what somebody did with those kinds of things.

New Skins Dresses

This case study and the one following are the product of two student workshops. One was at Pratt Institute in Brooklyn, New York, and the other was at the Metropolitan Exchange, also in Brooklyn, New York (Figures 4.15 and 4.16).

We sought to achieve two different things with these dresses. First, we wanted to see what the role of algorithm would be not only in thinking about material, but also in thinking about form, and how algorithms in computing can be used as a form-finding function. Second, we wanted to see what this would mean for the formal exploration, to create methods and modes of co-creation. We asked ourselves, "What does algorithm and computing mean for a future where product design is largely achieved through manipulation of digital means? Will it be a

FIGURE 4.15 New Skins workshop in Brooklyn. Photo by Chris Vongsawat.

FIGURE 4.16 New Skins workshop in Brooklyn. Photo by Chris Vongsawat.

piece of media, or multimedia, or an interactive experience of purchasing or designing the product?" This was really the kind of motivation for working through computing as a means of form finding.

The Verlan Dress

In the first course at Pratt Institute, we asked all the students to work with a body scan of a female model and a pre-programmed application. The pre-programmed application was designed to use Boids Flocking Algorithms. We asked the students to use that algorithm to explore what kinds of forms could engage with the body, and to think about what this might mean for fashion designers as an idea-generating tool. Building upon that, we asked the students to consider how that idea-generating tool might inform the way we think about the way products go to market, and how we might interact with the new emerging manufacturing infrastructures. In the case of the first dress, which used Boids flocking algorithm, there was a wide range of possible behaviors.

BOIDS

Boids flocking algorithm works discretely, like many of the algorithm systems outlined in this book. It simulates swarms of agents. The vector that the agents are traveling on is governed by the conditions surrounding the vector, and considers what other agents in its field of vision are doing. There are many variations on this and many variations by projects produced by our studio and of our students.

Flocking Systems (Algorithms)

Craig Reynolds pioneered flocking simulations in 1987, using clusters of simple agents, often referred to as "boids," to create patterns that simulate a flocking or swarm-like behavior. Flocking algorithms rely on three main principles: separation, alignment, and cohesion in a recursive process.

Boids

Boids, which is also the name of Craig Reynold's original simulation, represent the individual agents within the flocking algorithm. Each boid is its own object that contains information about its current position and direction of travel, and, in accumulation, each boid makes up the flock.

Separation

Separation describes the process of moving each boid away from its neighbors. Each boid draws a vector between its neighboring boids within a certain range to itself. The weighted average of the resulting vectors based on distance determines the direction of the boid in question. Separation allows boids to avoid collision with other boids.

Alignment

Alignment defines each boid's direction in relation to the flock. Each boid finds its neighboring boids within a certain range, measures the weighted average of all their respective directions of travel, and matches it.

Cohesion

Cohesion defines the process of finding the vector between each boid and the center of the flock.

Flocking System Algorithm

To execute a flocking algorithm, an array of boids is operated upon, using the alignment, cohesion and separation algorithms. These algorithms are given their own biases and strengths, producing a variety of different iterations.

In order to execute the alignment, cohesion, and separation algorithms, a function must be defined that returns all the boids that exist within a certain range of the boid being evaluated. With this function, we can loop through all the boids in question, find each one's corresponding neighbors, and calculate the result of the alignment, cohesion, or separation algorithms.

Once the overall direction of travel for each boid is determined from the summation of the alignment, cohesion, and separation output, the boids are moved once in that direction, and then the process is applied again onto the flock of new boids recursively.

We used these flocking algorithms to generate a volumetric pattern in our United Nude Collaboration. These patterns were used to create a negative volume that was subtracted from the base of the shoe. These patterns were all generated procedurally so that enabled us to generate a unique pattern each time someone ordered a shoe (Figures 4.17, 4.18, 4.19, and 4.20).

FIGURE 4.17 United Nude Collaboration.

FIGURE 4.18 United Nude Collaboration.

FIGURE 4.19 United Nude Collaboration.

FIGURE 4.20 United Nude Collaboration.

But all the variations that you see from the students' works that follow are just variations on those parameters, regarding each individual agent and the system's reaction to various context. Meaning, is there a predator nearby, or is one of my fellow agents in the area? And this is the underlying structure and principle that is responsible for all the variation in the designs. Geometric properties emerge from these interactions.

We gave all the students the same algorithm, the same body scan, and essentially the same material to work with, yet they all produced wildly different results. And we were encouraged by their answers, which went beyond just customizable products. These results go a long way to dispel the myth that computation produces homogenous design results. You can see in the accompanying images all the sketches, variations, and the extremely different outputs that came from the same system (Figure 4.21). In the end, we asked the students to choose one single dress design, materialize it, and work together to construct that dress. We called this dress the Verlan because *verlan* is the French word for transposing syllables within a word to create a slang term. The Verlan Dress created networks around the model's body (Figures 4.22 and 4.23).

FIGURE 4.21 New Skins workshop.

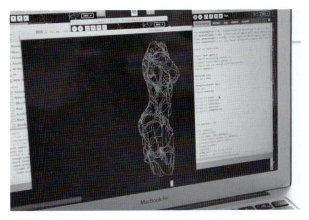

FIGURE 4.22 New Skins workshop simulation.

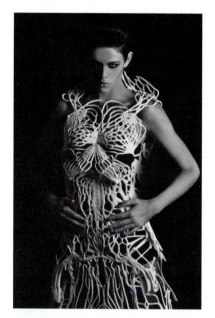

FIGURE 4.23 Verlan Dress. Photograph by CHRISTRINI.

At the time, we were working in collaboration with MakerBot, testing out a new flexible polyester-based filament. We printed it in many parts on a desktop 3D printer, and assembled the final product with heat. We had used a polymer filament that had a very low melting point, so we printed the parts independently and used heat to fuse the parts into one seamless design.

The Bristle Dress

The second project we did with this group of students resulted in the creation of the Bristle Dress, and involved a different procedure and algorithm. With this dress, we wanted to have the students work with a branching system. This time, we were interested to see how the students would confront the issue of materiality.

The Verlan Dress was designed in a digital environment and was very difficult to fabricate. If you download the files and try to print it yourself, you'll see the difficulty. In contrast, the Bristle Dress prints largely without support. Though it is difficult to assemble, it's not as challenging as the Verlan Dress. We designed each component of the Bristle Dress to be printed on desktop technology, whereas the Verlan Dress was more or less designed in a vacuum (Figures 4.24 and 4.25).

I want to talk about these two projects together because they represent a learning experience, where the two systems inform each other. Though it is empowering to think about material constructions as digital media, there is still a material component. These algorithms are different from producing

FIGURE 4.24 Bristle Dress concept rendering.

FIGURE 4.25 Bristle Dress. Photograph
by Chris Vongsawat.

systems for visualizations of film media. They need to be
informed by the material constraints of the tool in order to
make meaningful experiences. On the one hand, we can take
advantage of the emerging distributed manufacturing
infrastructures that we talked about earlier in this book. On
the other hand, if we cannot use these tools to extend our
capacities and produce more complex things more easily, then
we will not unlock the full potential of the tools.

Mostly what this workshop produced were actually failed
prints of the Bristle Dress. We tried different settings to find the
limits of what the printer could print. We wanted to know how
far we could push the desktop printer, in this case a MakerBot,
before it failed.

And we had very surprising results. We found that certain geometries would correct themselves over time. They initially failed—we produced much deeper overhangs than we had thought. Many of these failures had to do with different aspects of the geometries, and it required an enormous amount of testing to correct. We spent two weeks testing different geometries in the same system so we could define final parameters that would achieve the most rapid production possible.

Interestingly, in this line of research, we found that some of the failures were actually quite beautiful. After this realization, we started to expand our investigation by allowing the tool to move off the path of the intended geometry, at some point producing emerging effects in the material. These flocking algorithms produced emerging effects in the geometries themselves.

The hood of the Bristle Dress was created through the branching algorithm. The entire hood is made up of thousands and thousands of unique nodes. All of them worked, and none failed in the printer. The assembly went very smoothly because we were able to calculate the printer's output at a small scale. As a result, we were able to do an enormous amount of rapid testing on what appears to be an incredibly complex construction that is actually very simple.

The skirt on the bottom, we learned, was not informed very much by what we had developed on the Verlan Dress. If you go through the CAD files associated with this project, you would see that all the components were designed to be printed flat and each one of the angles was mitered, so you could press each end of a faceted panel against the other. Apply heat, and the dress would fuse together seamlessly. It is a system of panels designed to fit inside of a desktop printer that could be assembled into a skirt.

When we uploaded the skirt to Thingiverse, we released it as a customizable entity. We put an applet in the skirt's description, and this opened up another interesting conversation. People would now not only be able to customize the skirt to fit them, or affect the flare or silhouette before printing, but they could also save that design and share it with others.

After we released the Bristle Dress and the course was over, the line between social networking and design really started to blur. The Verlan Dress was generated purely through procedural algorithm, and customers could edit those settings, share them, store them, and rank them, just like you could do in other kinds of social-media-based ecommerce platforms. I think this presents an interesting potential in terms of the future of anticipative buying and passive customization. Not everybody may have time to design a dress like this, but there could be an open-sourced component to this that informs the design in real time as it is out in the marketplace. This was a very interesting emergent and second property of this dress (Figures 4.26 and 4.27).

FIGURE 4.26 Bristle Dress. Photograph by Chris Vongsawat.

FIGURE 4.27 Bristle Dress. Photograph by Chris Vongsawat.

It is important to note this dress and the other case studies in this book are not fantastic works or singular artistic acts of creation. These works are setting the stage for the potential of 3D printing technology. We are only just starting to understand the material capabilities, material limits, and how to design for this technology.

Both the Verlan Dress and the Bristle Dress are available for you to download on Thingiverse (search: verlan dress thingiverse / bristle dress thingiverse).

Scoliosis Brace with UNYQ

Following on from the design of these three dresses, it seemed pertinent to ask what fields and applications could really benefit from the 3D printing process? Specifically in empowering the consumer to generate his or her own product.

In this regard, we fell upon the following project: designing a Scoliosis Brace with UNYQ (a medical orthopedics design company in San Franciscio).

There is so much that additive manufacturing can add to the medical field for obvious reasons. 3D printing provides a way to manufacture customized products on a large scale, an ability that traditional forms of manufacturing simply cannot compete with. The medical field is the quintessential example of a practice that requires this kind of mass customization as it requires interaction with a patient's body, a match that is unique to every person.

Additionally, the field is full of outdated, ad hoc and often dehumanizing solutions to complex situations. In many cases, this is, of course, a product of a field that often depends on traditional manufacturing. This problem with production is obvious with regards to scoliosis treatment.

INTERVIEW WITH LES KARPAS, PREVIOUSLY FOUNDER AND CEO OF METAMASON, AND CURRENT CEO OF LEXSET

Discovering the crucial need for technological innovation in the healthcare sector was a major catalytic force for founding Metamason (Figure 4.28). I synthesized my experience with machine vision, 3D printers, manufacturing engineering, and the use of smart geometry: the core of the company is a virtual Scan·Fit·Print[SM] platform for creating individually personalized products with automated fabrication equipment for the medical devices industry. By merging 3D scans of the user's face with our proprietary technique for 3D printed biocompatible silicone, our devices are uniquely patient-matched and user-oriented. I believe

FIGURE 4.28 Les Karpas.

strongly that 3D integration and automation like ours will revolutionize the world of design, for personalized medicine and beyond.

The success of patient-matched products like Invisalign braces and 3D printed hearing aids is already being demonstrated, both in terms of popularity and improved efficacy. Designers of customized prosthetics and orthopedics, like Scott Summit of Bespoke Innovations and Eythor Bender of UNYQ, have clinically proven the positive psychological effects of the patient's actual body and personal style being represented through the device. For an example, take a look at what e-Nable has done with Disney- and Marvel-themed prosthetic limbs for children, and how much more happy and accepted it makes those children feel. By giving the patient agency in the design and creation of a personalized product, the product becomes an extension of the patient's identity—and patient activation through product personalization consistently improves outcomes through increased compliance. More simply put, our medical devices should be extensions of our bodies which enhance and enable, not restraints that infirm.

Few truly effective therapies suffer from noncompliance as egregious as Continuous Positive Airway Pressure (CPAP). Over 25 million Americans suffer from Obstructive Sleep Apnea (OSA), a dangerous chronic condition in which the airway is partially obstructed during sleep. [It has been found that] 1 in 4 men and 1 in 9 women experience oxygen deprivation and sleep disturbance dozens or even hundreds of times per night, causing physiological stress and chronic fatigue. OSA can lead to diminished neurocognitive function, increased risk of motor-vehicle accidents, reduced quality of life, hypertension, insulin resistance, and cardiovascular diseases. Left untreated, OSA dramatically increases the likelihood of depression, erectile dysfunction, diabetes, stroke, and early mortality. Unfortunately, roughly 50 percent of OSA patients quit the prescribed therapy (CPAP) within the first year, reporting discomfort due to poor fit of mass-produced masks as the leading cause for noncompliance. Despite myriad attempts to provide new solutions for unsatisfied patients, the sustained attrition and noncompliance statistics associated with CPAP therapy bely a failure to address the core cause of poor fit. All CPAP masks currently offered by the aforementioned companies are made using conventional injection molding and are only available in a few generic sizes.

I witnessed first-hand the serious implications of CPAP noncompliance. My father struggled with respiratory issues before his premature death, and I remember his complaints about the discomfort and indignity of his ill-fitting CPAP mask, which led him to stop using the therapy. Ignoring CPAP undoubtedly accelerated his illness and diminished his quality of life in the time he had left. When I learned that CPAP noncompliance is exceptionally common, and that a better-fitting mask could potentially save tens of thousands of lives each year, it seemed to be a problem I was uniquely poised to solve. I researched CPAP therapy and began applying my background in 3D scanning, modeling, and custom fabrication to develop a better-fitting solution for CPAP patients.

Every human face is different. I believe that individualized fit is essential for CPAP therapy to be genuinely effective. With our innovative patient-matched approach and proprietary production process, Metamason is the first company to bring true customization via 3D printing to the respiratory space (Figure 4.29).

Our Scan·Fit·Print process integrates 3D scan data and cutting-edge ergonomic design to engineer perfect body conformity. Each patient-matched product is manufactured on demand. Cost-effective 3D customization for CPAP is only recently possible because of diverse technological maturity, the alchemy of Metamason's in-house expertise, and our patented process inventions. Miia™ is the world's first CPAP product individually designed for every patient; each patient-matched Miia mask offers comfort, flexibility, and immediate flawless fit (Figure 4.30).

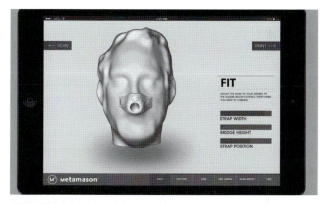

FIGURE 4.29 MetaMason software.

FIGURE 4.30 MetaMason Miia mask.

I've been captivated by 3D printing since I was a kid (I started modeling at age 12 in 1993, and printing interning for architecture firms in 1999). The more I experimented, the more I believed that the possibilities for this technology were truly limitless; and the more I learned about the current manufacturing industry, the more I realized that the conventional systems for designing and mass-producing products weren't going to assimilate emerging 3D technology very effectively, or engage its true capacity. Our tools and process have evolved from a world focused on mass production, and are fundamentally misaligned with the needs of mass customization. The way we *think* about design and manufacturing needs a philosophical overhaul in order to leverage these technologies to their full potential.

This realization has inspired me to explore what that design philosophy might look like for mass customization, and ultimately to define and describe it as Metamodernism. Metamodernism is a scan-to-fit design philosophy for the fourth industrial revolution, which unites 3D technology with modernist pedagogy to enable mass customization. From the moment I began framing discussions of design process this way with my peers and colleagues, something clicked, and the idea began to gain traction.

If a product isn't produced until it has a user, that means its design is incomplete until the user is included. In this way, Metamodernism is about metaproducts: products that have an essence and a function, but no form without the individual they're meant for.

Through spreading a Metamodernist ideology, my hope is to enable businesses and entrepreneurs to better leverage 3D technology to capture emerging market opportunities and reimagine product design. I hope that eventually, C-level executives of the future can say, "I think we should take a Metamodernist approach to this market."

As designers of patient-matched products, Metamason takes data in, manipulates that data by applying algorithms, and giving it purpose, and then pushes it back out into the world. The real power is in automating that process. That means creating pipelines that make the tech "just work." Yes, we have created parametric meta-designs that are fluid and data-sensitive—but we're also developing a Scan·Fit·Print app that puts our integrated design process directly in the hands of doctors and patients. Ultimately— even in the case of complex and specialized medical devices like ours—the user shouldn't be thinking about the technology being used to create the content; they're thinking about the content they want to create.

Scoliosis is a deformation of the spine in relation to the hips. The severity of the deformation is described by the "cobb angle," which measures the angle of deformation between the highest vertebrae and lowest vertebrae of the scoliosis curve.

Currently, physicians deal with this curvature by applying a custom brace with padding at specific areas that apply force to correct the spine's curvature. These custom braces are made by wrapping a heated medical plastic around a patient's torso, and applying higher and higher forces until the patient's spine is straightened. The problem with this ad hoc approach is that it results in an inefficient, uncomfortable, physically limiting, and unappealing brace design that may embarrass patients, who are typically adolescents.

Our method for approaching this problem was to address the inefficiencies of vacuum forming a medical plastic on a patient by replacing it with an SLS printing process.

Our 3D printed design focused on creating an appealing form that could empower the patient to make his or her own design choices while simultaneously reducing weight and allowing for more mobility/comfort. To meet some of these goals, we first ran the current brace design through a topology optimization process.

With technology like this, a mass like the brace can be transformed into a shape like the one shown in Figures 4.31, 4.32, and 4.33.

At the human scale of a product, these often complex forms are difficult to obtain through typical manufacturing methods. This is, in fact, the second opportunity (after mass customization) that additive manufacturing provides in advancing the designs of medical devices.

Sensors placed in the brace helped us accurately measure the magnitude of the applied loads, giving us input for the topology optimization process. The brace design also incorporates a lifetime sensor placed in the back, giving us

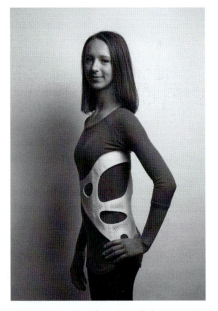

FIGURE 4.31 Photograph by Jason Perry.

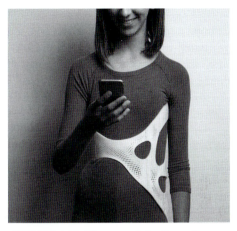

FIGURE 4.32 Photograph by Jason Perry.

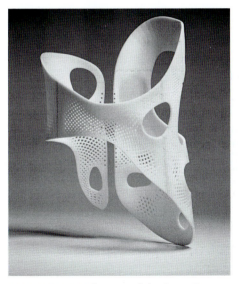

FIGURE 4.33 Photograph by Jason Perry.

real-time feedback on its use and efficiency over time. With this feedback, we hope to generate superior designs in the future.

After the original brace was reduced, we ran the topology optimization a second time, but now, instead of removing mass, we applied a pattern that changed, based on parts of the brace that the topology optimization deemed removable.

The system applied to the form is based on structural necessity, but the input pattern is chosen by the user, who is given a menu of patterns to select. This last step in the design process really speaks to the nature of the project. While the application of the user-selected pattern is functional, allowing for further weight reduction and porosity, it is also a human-centered approach, empowering the patient to have a say in how he or she is treated. All of this is only feasible through additive manufacturing (Figure 4.34).

FIGURE 4.34 Photograph by Jason Perry.

The outcome of this design process produced a customizable product that meets all structural requirements and will adapt over time. But the final results not only look better, but are also more flexible, more comfortable, and over 50–75 percent lighter than the original design.

Conclusion

It is my hope that this book provides future designers with a source of inspiration and a launching point for future work. While producing this work it has been fascinating for me and I feel privileged to have been able to work on these projects at such an early stage of 3D printing and generative design. This work takes time to evolve and it will take a whole generation for designers to fully master these design methodologies and build an intuition for the types of materials, structures, and forms that are possible. I do believe that 3D printing will give us an entire new design vocabulary and open up a class of products and experiences that have never been possible before. I hope that people will read this work and pick up where we have left off. I have done my best to be candid about my own experiences and provide a full picture of the processes used to create these works. I am confident that 3D printing will bring us a brighter, more sustainable future and that it will be the next generation of designers who fully unlock that potential.

Conclusion

I hope that this book has framed a new approach to materials and thinking about how materials are formed and shaped. As a result of these technologies, materials themselves are relational and linguistic. The 3D printer is a universal platform for the formation of matter that can be controlled by language and is capable of being networked. 3D printers are capable of producing so much variety because they run on a discrete additive logic. It is a generic non-specific tool, capable of self-replication. 3D printers present us with a methodology for thinking about materials and assemblies as a set of discretized operations that inform a manipulation of matter that is much closer to how we manipulate software; and as a result, assembly of physical form and material differentiation no longer fall on the tool but on the manipulation of a codified language. This is a paradigm shift. This means materials are now shaped by linguistic constructs (computer programing languages), rather than formations of other materials.

For the first time ever, our tools are linguistic. Language is now our hammer and saw. This means product design, architecture, and fashion design are now all social activities, capable of benefiting from the distributed models we have seen emerge since the dawn of the Internet. Materials are flexible, malleable things, capable of being formed, shared, and edited in a digital environment. We can remix objects, materials become like a video or a song. In the dawn of this new age, material is media.

INDEX

Page numbers in **bold** refer to figures.